when Granny meets Filet™

Introduction

This is a pick-and-choose book. Pick your favorite granny squares and filet pieces from the numerous options and then choose your yarn colors for unique, one-of-a-kind designs.

YARN
The granny squares, filet pieces and all of the designs in this book were created using:

Berroco Comfort DK light (DK) weight yarn, (1¾ oz/178 yds/50g per ball).

Berroco Comfort DK comes in 38 solids and 11 prints, giving a total of 49 colors to choose from.

The 21 colors used in this book include:

#2702 pearl	#2703 barley
#2719 sunshine	#2720 hummus
#2721 sprig	#2722 purple
#2723 rosebud	#2726 cornflower
#2730 teaberry	#2731 kidz orange
#2733 turquoise	#2734 liquorice
#2736 primary blue	#2740 seedling
#2742 pimpernel	#2745 filbert

#2748 Aunt Martha green

#2751 true red

#2754 rabe

#2758 crypto crystalline

#2813 multi brights

CROCHET HOOK
F/5/3.75mm crochet hook.

GAUGE
Granny squares, before edgings are added, are 3¾-inch squares. Use any size hook needed to obtain gauge.

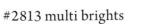

DESIGNER TOUCH 1

If sewing squares together where no edging will be added, after last round is completed, fasten off, leaving a long strand of yarn for sewing.

DESIGNER TOUCH 2

On any round that ends with a chain and then a join, if one doesn't want the final join to be obvious, one can omit the last chain and join then work as follows:

Leaving loop on hook, fasten off yarn, leaving a 6-inch strand. Pull loop on hook up until yarn end comes through stitch. Insert hook, from back to front, through both loops of the stitch or chain that you are instructed to join in; using hook, pull yarn end through loops. Insert hook, from bottom to top of back loop of last stitch or chain made on round; using hook, pull yarn end through stitch. This forms the last chain and also the join.

DESIGNER TOUCH 3

To save weaving time, crochet over yarn ends whenever possible.

DESIGNER TOUCH 4

Squares can be sewn together using a variety of methods.

For the designs in this book, unless specific directions are given, use your method of choice.

The squares in the book were sewn together by placing 2 squares together with right sides facing; using outer loops of stitches and chains, pieces were whipstitched together.

DESIGNER TOUCH 5

All Granny Squares in this book have 15 stitches and or chains on each side and 3 chains in each corner on their last round making them interchangeable. ■

GRANNY SQUARE 1

PATTERN NOTES
Uses 4 colors.

To turn Granny Square into full-size afghan, repeat round 2 until afghan is 1 round less than desired size, then work round 4 pulling chain-10 spaces of every round through ch spaces of previous round.

Join with slip stitch as indicated unless otherwise stated.

Chain-3 at beginning of row or round counts as first double crochet unless otherwise stated.

INSTRUCTIONS
SQUARE
Rnd 1 (RS): With first color, ch 4, sl st in first ch to form ring, **ch 3** (*see Pattern Notes*), 4 dc in ring, ch 7, [5 dc in ring, ch 7] 3 times, **join** (*see Pattern Notes*) in 3rd ch of beg ch-3. Fasten off.

Rnd 2: With RS facing, join 2nd color in first dc, ch 3, dc in same ch as beg ch 3, *dc in each st across to last st before next ch sp, 2 dc in last st, ch 10, sk next ch sp**, 2 dc in next st, rep from * around, ending last rep at **, join in 3rd ch of beg ch-3. Fasten off.

Rnd 3: With 3rd color, rep rnd 2.

Rnd 4: Pull ch-10 sp on rnd 2 through ch-7 sp on rnd 1, pull ch-10 sp of rnd 3 through ch-10 sp of rnd 2, with RS facing, join 4th color with sc in ch-10 sp of rnd 3, *3 dc in first dc on this side, dc in each st across to last st before next ch-10 sp, 3 dc in last st**, (sc, ch 3, sc) in ch-10 sp, rep from * around, ending last rep at **, sc in same ch-10 sp as joining sc, ch 3, join in joining sc. Fasten off. ■

GRANNY SQUARE 2

Chain-4 at beginning of row or round counts as first double crochet and chain-1 unless otherwise stated.

INSTRUCTIONS
SQUARE

Rnd 1 (RS): With first color, ch 4, sl st in first ch to form ring, **ch 4** (*see Pattern Notes*), [(dc, ch 3, dc, ch 1) in ring (*corner*), ch 1] 3 times, dc in ring, ch 3 (*corner*), **join** (*see Pattern Notes*) in 3rd ch of beg ch-4. Fasten off.

Rnd 2: With RS facing, join 2nd color in any corner ch-3 sp, ch 4, *[dc in next dc, ch 1] twice**, (dc, ch 3, dc) in next corner ch-3 sp, ch 1, rep from * around, ending last rep at **, dc in same corner ch sp as beg ch-4, ch 3, join in 3rd ch of beg ch-4. Fasten off.

Rnd 3: With RS facing, join 3rd color in any corner ch-3 sp, ch 4, *[dc in next dc, ch 1] across to next corner ch-3 sp**, (dc, ch 3, dc) in corner ch-3 sp, ch 1, rep from * around, ending last rep at **, dc in same ch sp as beg ch-4, ch 3, join in 3rd ch of beg ch-4. Fasten off.

Rnd 4: With 4th color, rep rnd 3. ∎

PATTERN NOTES
Uses 4 colors.

To turn Granny Square into full-size afghan, repeat round 3 until afghan is desired size.

Join with slip stitch as indicated unless otherwise stated.

GRANNY SQUARE 3

INSTRUCTIONS
SQUARE

Rnd 1 (RS): With first color, ch 4, sl st in first ch to form ring, **ch 4** (*see Pattern Notes*), [dc in ring, ch 1] 7 times, **join** (*see Pattern Notes*) in 3rd ch of beg ch-4. Fasten off.

Rnd 2: With RS facing, join 2nd color in any ch-1 sp, **ch 3** (*see Pattern Notes*), dc in same ch sp as beg ch-3, *2 **fptr** (*see Stitch Guide*) around next dc, ch 1**, 2 dc in next ch-1 sp, rep from * around, ending last rep at **, join in 3rd ch of beg ch-3. Fasten off.

Rnd 3: With RS facing, join 3rd color in first dc of any dc group, ch 3, dc in same dc as beg ch-3, *ch 1, 2 dc in next dc, ch 1, sk next 2 fptr, 2 tr in next dc, ch 3 (*corner*), 2 tr in next st, ch 1, sk next 2 fptr**, 2 dc in next dc, rep from * around, ending last rep at **, join in 3rd ch of beg ch-3. Fasten off.

Rnd 4: With RS facing, join 4th color in any corner ch-3 sp, ch 4, dc in same corner ch sp as beg ch-4, *(dc, ch 1, dc) in each of next 3 ch-1 sps**, (dc, ch 1, dc, ch 3, dc, ch 1, dc) in next corner ch-3 sp, rep from * around, ending last rep at **, (dc, ch 1, dc, ch 3) in same ch sp as beg ch-4, join in 3rd ch of beg ch-4. Fasten off. ∎

PATTERN NOTES

Uses 4 colors.

Join with slip stitch as indicated unless otherwise stated.

Chain-4 at beginning of row or round counts as first double crochet and chain-1 unless otherwise stated.

Chain-3 at beginning of row or round counts as first double crochet unless otherwise stated.

GRANNY SQUARE 4

PATTERN NOTES
Uses 3 colors.

Join with slip stitch as indicated unless otherwise stated.

Chain-5 at beginning of row or round counts as first double crochet and chain-2 unless otherwise stated.

Chain-3 at beginning of row or round counts as first double crochet unless otherwise stated.

SPECIAL STITCHES
Beginning double crochet cluster (beg dc cl): Ch 2, holding back last lp of each st on hook, 2 dc as indicated in instructions, yo, pull through all lps on hook.

Double crochet cluster (dc cl): Holding back last lp of each st on hook, 3 dc as indicated in instructions, yo, pull through all lps on hook.

Beginning treble crochet cluster (beg tr cl): Ch 3, holding back last lp of each st on hook, 2 tr as indicated in instructions, yo, pull through all lps on hook.

Treble crochet cluster (tr cl): Holding back last lp of each st on hook, 3 tr as indicated in instructions, yo, pull through all lps on hook.

INSTRUCTIONS
SQUARE
Rnd 1 (RS): With first color, ch 4, sl st in first ch to form ring, **ch 3** (see Pattern Notes), 15 dc in ring, **join** (see Pattern Notes) in 3rd ch of beg ch-3. Fasten off. (16 dc)

Rnd 2: With RS facing, join 2nd color in any dc, **beg dc cl** (see Special Stitches) in same st, [ch 4, sk next st, **dc cl** (see Special Stitches) in next st] 7 times, ch 4, join in top of beg dc cl. Fasten off. (8 dc cls)

Rnd 3: With RS facing, join 3rd color in any ch-4 sp, **beg tr cl** (see Special Stitches) in same ch sp as beg ch-3, *ch 2, 5 dc in next ch-4 sp, ch 2**, (**tr cl**—see Special Stitches, ch 3, tr cl) in next ch-4 sp (corner), rep from * around, ending last rep at **, tr cl in same ch sp as beg tr cl, ch 2, join with sc in top of beg tr cl, forming last ch sp. **Do not fasten off.**

Rnd 4: Ch 5 (see Pattern Notes), *dc dec (see Stitch Guide) in next tr cl and next ch, ch 3, dc dec in next 5 dc, ch 3, dc dec in next tr cl and next ch, ch 2**, (dc, ch 3, dc) in next corner ch sp, ch 2, rep from * around, ending last rep at **, dc in same ch sp as beg ch-5, ch 3, join in 3rd ch of beg ch-5. Fasten off. ∎

GRANNY SQUARE 5

PATTERN NOTES

Uses 4 colors.

To turn into full-size afghan, repeat round 4 to desired size.

Join with slip stitch as indicated unless otherwise stated.

Chain-3 at beginning of row or round counts as first double crochet unless otherwise stated.

INSTRUCTIONS
SQUARE

Rnd 1 (RS): With first color, ch 4, sl st in first ch to form ring, **ch 3** (see Pattern Notes), 2 dc in ring, [ch 3 (corner), 3 dc in ring] 3 times, ch 3, **join** (see Pattern Notes) in 3rd ch of beg ch-3. Fasten off.

Rnd 2: With RS facing, join 2nd color in any corner ch-3 sp, ch 3, (2 dc, ch 3, 3 dc) in same corner ch sp as beg ch-3, [ch 1, (3 dc, ch 3, 3 dc) in next corner ch-3 sp] around, ch 1, join in 3rd ch of beg ch-3. Fasten off.

Rnd 3: With RS facing, join 3rd color in any corner ch-3 sp, ch 3, (2 dc, ch 3, 3 dc) in same corner ch sp as beg ch-3, *ch 1, 3 dc in next ch-1 sp, ch 1**, (3 dc, ch 3, 3 dc) in next corner ch-3 sp, rep from * around, ending last rep at **, join in 3rd ch of beg ch-3. Fasten off.

Rnd 4: With RS facing, join 4th color in any corner ch-3 sp, ch 3, (2 dc, ch 3, 3 dc) in same corner ch sp as beg ch-3, *[ch 1, 3 dc in next ch-1 sp] across to next corner ch sp, ch 1**, (3 dc, ch 3, 3 dc) in next corner ch sp, rep from * around, ending last rep at **, join in 3rd ch of beg ch-3. Fasten off. ∎

GRANNY SQUARE 6

PATTERN NOTES

Uses 2 colors.

When using 2 colors alternately, to save weaving time, do not fasten off at end of round. Instead, on round 1, using first color, work round, join in beginning stitch, drop loop from hook, pull dropped loop through beginning stitch to back of work. For round 2, join 2nd color in next corner chain-3 space to the left, work round, join in beginning stitch, drop loop from hook, pull dropped loop through beginning st to back of work. For round 3, insert hook in corner chain-3 space to the right, pick up dropped loop of first color (*dropped loop will be a little to the left of the corner chain-3 space*), pull dropped loop through chain-3 space, bringing it up even with current round, then begin round. For 4th round, insert hook in corner chain-3 space to the left, pick up dropped lp of 2nd color (*dropped loop will be a little to the left of the corner chain-3 space*), pull dropped loop through chain-3 space, bringing it up even with current round, then begin round. For additional rounds, alternate method used for rounds 3 and 4.

Join with slip stitch as indicated unless otherwise stated.

Chain-3 at beginning of row or round counts as first double crochet unless otherwise stated.

INSTRUCTIONS
SQUARE

Rnd 1 (WS): With first color, ch 4, sl st in first ch to form ring, **ch 3** (*see Pattern Notes*), 2 dc in ring, [ch 3 (*corner*), 3 dc in ring] 3 times, ch 3, **join** (*see Pattern Notes*) in 3rd ch of beg ch-3. Fasten off.

Rnd 2 (RS): With RS facing, join 2nd color in any corner ch-3 sp, ch 3, 2 dc in same ch sp as beg ch-3, [ch 1, (3 dc, ch 3, 3 dc) in next corner ch-3 sp] around, ch 1, 3 dc in same corner ch sp as beg ch-3, ch 3, join in 3rd ch of beg ch-3. Fasten off.

Rnd 3: With RS facing, join first color with sc in any corner ch-3 sp, 2 sc in same corner ch sp as joining sc, *ch 1, sc in next ch-1 sp, **fpdtr** (*see Stitch Guide*) around 2nd dc of dc group on rnd 1, sc in same ch-1 sp as last sc on this rnd, ch 1**, (3 sc, ch 3, 3 sc) in next corner ch-3 sp, rep from * around, ending last rep at **, 3 sc in same corner ch sp as joining sc, ch 3, join in beg sc. Fasten off.

Rnd 4: With RS facing, join 2nd color in any corner ch-3 sp, ch 3, 2 dc in same corner ch sp as beg ch-3, *[ch 1, 2 dc in next ch-1 sp] twice, ch 1**, (3 dc, ch 3, 3 dc) in next corner ch-3 sp, rep from * around, ending last rep at **, 3 dc in same corner ch-3 sp as beg ch-3, ch 3, join in 3rd ch of beg ch-3. Fasten off.

Rnd 5: With RS facing, join first color with sc in any corner ch-3 sp, ch 1, sc in same ch sp as joining sc, *sc in each of next 3 dc, **fptr** (*see Stitch Guide*) around 2nd sc of sc group on rnd 3, sc in each of next 2 dc, sc in next ch-1 sp, sc in each of next 2 dc, fptr around 2nd sc in sc group on rnd 3, sc in each of next 3 dc**, (sc, ch 3, sc) in next corner ch-3 sp, rep from * around, ending last rep at **, sc in same corner ch sp as joining sc, ch 3, join in beg sc. Fasten off. ■

GRANNY SQUARE 7

PATTERN NOTES

Uses 2 colors.

Alternate 2 colors throughout.

Work over dropped color where indicated.

Change colors in last st made.

Join with slip stitch as indicated unless otherwise stated.

Chain-3 at beginning of round counts as first double crochet unless otherwise stated.

INSTRUCTIONS
SQUARE

Rnd 1 (WS): With first color, ch 4, sl st in first ch to form ring, **ch 3** (*see Pattern Notes*), 2 dc in ring, ch 3 (*corner*), 3 dc in ring, **changing color** (*see Stitch Guide and Pattern Notes*) in last st, ch 3, working over dropped color, 3 dc in ring, ch 3, without working over dropped color, 3 dc in ring, ch 1, join with dc in 3rd ch of beg ch-3, forming last ch sp, **turn.**

Rnd 2 (RS): Ch 3, 2 dc in same ch sp as beg ch-3, *ch 1, (3 dc, ch 3, 3 dc) in next corner ch-3 sp, ch 1, *bring dropped color up to next ch-3 sp so that it can be worked over, working over dropped color, (3 dc, changing color, ch 3, 3 dc) in next corner ch sp, rep between * once, 3 dc in same corner ch sp as beg ch-3, ch 1, join with dc in 3rd ch of beg ch-3, forming last ch sp, turn.

Rnd 3 (WS): Ch 3, 2 dc in same ch sp as beg ch-3, *ch 1, 3 dc in next ch-1 sp, ch 1, (3 dc, ch 3, 3 dc) in next corner ch sp, ch 1, 3 dc in next ch-1 sp, ch 1*, bring dropped color up to next corner ch sp so that it can be worked over, working over dropped color, (3 dc, changing color, ch 3, 3 dc) in next corner ch sp, rep between * once, 3 dc in same ch sp as beg ch-3, ch 1, join with dc in 3rd ch of beg ch-3, turn.

Rnd 4 (RS): Ch 3, 2 dc in same corner ch sp as beg ch-3, *[ch 1, 3 dc in next ch-1 sp] twice, ch 1, (3 dc, ch 3, 3 dc) in next corner ch sp, [ch 1, 3 dc in next ch-1 sp] twice, ch 1*, bring dropped color up to next corner ch sp so that it can be worked over, working over dropped color, (3 dc, changing color, ch 3, 3 dc) in next corner ch sp, rep between * once, 3 dc in same ch sp as beg ch-3, ch 3, **join** (*see Pattern Notes*) in 3rd ch of beg ch-3. Fasten off both colors. ■

GRANNY SQUARE 8

PATTERN NOTES
Uses 8 colors.

Join with slip stitch as indicated unless otherwise stated.

SPECIAL STITCH
Tall single crochet (tall sc): Insert hook as indicated in instructions, yo, pull lp through, yo, pull through 1 lp on hook, yo, pull through 2 lps on hook.

INSTRUCTIONS
SQUARE

Rnd 1 (RS): With first color, ch 4, sl st in first ch to form ring, ch 1, 8 sc in ring, **join** (see Pattern Notes) in beg sc. Fasten off.

Rnd 2: With RS facing, join 2nd color in any st, ch 1, **tall sc** (see Special Stitch) in same st as joining sl st, ch 1, [tall sc in next st, ch 1] around, join in top of beg tall sc. Fasten off.

Rnd 3: With RS facing, join 3rd color with sc in any ch-1 sp, sc in same ch sp as joining sc, *ch 1, 2 sc in next ch-1 sp, ch 3 (corner)**, 2 sc in next ch-1 sp, rep from * around, ending last rep at **, join in joining sc. Fasten off.

Rnd 4: With RS facing, join 4th color with sc in any corner ch-3 sp, sc in same corner ch sp as joining sc, *ch 1, tall sc in next ch-1 sp, ch 1**, (2 sc, ch 3, 2 sc) in next corner ch-3 sp, rep from * around, ending last rep at **, 2 sc in same ch sp as joining sc, ch 3, join in joining sc. Fasten off.

Rnd 5: With RS facing, join 5th color with sc in any corner ch-3 sp, sc in same ch sp as joining sc, *[ch 1, tall sc in next ch-1 sp] across, ch 1**, (2 sc, ch 3, 2 sc) in next corner ch-3 sp, rep from * around, ending last rep at **, 2 sc in same corner as joining sc, ch 3, join in joining sc. Fasten off.

Rnds 6–8: Using 5th, 6th and 7th colors, rep rnd 5. ∎

GRANNY SQUARE 9

PATTERN NOTES

Uses 4 colors.

Join with slip stitch as indicated unless otherwise stated.

INSTRUCTIONS
SQUARE
STAMEN

Rnd 1 (RS): With color for Stamen, ch 4, sl st in first ch to form ring, [ch 3, sl st in **back bar** (*see illustration*) of 2nd ch from hook and in last ch, sl st in ring] 4 times. (*4 Stamens*)

Back Bar of Chain

Rnd 2: Push Stamen to center, [working behind Stamen, ch 1, sl st in ring] 4 times. Fasten off.

PETAL

Rnd 1: Join Petal color in any ch-1 sp, ch 1, (sc, dc, tr, dc) in same ch sp as beg ch-1, (sc, dc, tr, dc) in each ch-1 sp around, join in joining sc. (*4 petals*)

Rnd 2: Push Petals to center, working behind Petals, ch 2, [sl st in back of next sc, ch 2] around.

Rnd 3: Sl st in first ch-2 sp, ch 1, (sc, dc, tr, dc, sc, dc, tr, dc) in same ch sp as beg ch-1, (sc, dc, tr, dc, sc, dc, tr, dc) in each ch-2 sp around, **join** (*see Pattern Notes*) in back of joining sc. (*8 petals*)

Rnd 4: Push Petals to center, working behind Petals, [ch 3, sl st in back of next sc, ch 1, sl st in back of next sc] around. Fasten off.

LEAVES

Join Leaf color in any ch-3 sp, ch 4 (*counts as first tr*), (tr, ch 3, 2 tr) in same ch sp as beg ch-4 (*corner*), *ch 1, 2 tr in next ch-1 sp, ch 1**, (2 tr, ch 3, 2 tr) in next ch-3 sp (*corner*), rep from * around, ending last rep at **, join in 4th ch of beg ch-4. Fasten off.

BACKGROUND

Join Background color in any corner ch-3 sp, ch 3 (*counts as first dc*), (2 dc, ch 3, 3 dc) in same ch sp as beg ch-3, *[ch 1, 3 dc in next ch-1 sp] twice, ch 1**, (3 dc, ch 3, 3 dc) in next corner ch-3 sp, rep from * around, ending last rep at **, join in 3rd ch of beg ch-3. Fasten off. ∎

GRANNY SQUARE 10

PATTERN NOTES
Uses 4 colors.

To make full-size afghan, repeat round 3 until desired size.

Join with slip stitch as indicated unless otherwise stated.

Chain-3 at beginning of row or round counts as first double crochet unless otherwise stated.

INSTRUCTIONS
SQUARE
Rnd 1 (RS): With first color, ch 4, sl st in first ch to form ring, **ch 3** *(see Pattern Notes)*, 2 dc in ring, [ch 3 *(corner)*, 3 dc in ring] 3 times, ch 3 *(corner)*, join in 3rd ch of beg ch-3. Fasten off.

Rnd 2: With RS facing, join 2nd color in any corner ch-3 sp, ch 3, *fptr *(see Stitch Guide)* around first dc of dc group, dc in same dc as fptr, fptr around next dc, dc in last dc of dc group, fptr around same dc as last dc worked**, (dc, ch 3, dc) in next corner ch sp, rep from * around, ending last rep at **, dc in same ch sp as beg ch-3, ch 3, **join** *(see Pattern Notes)* in 3rd ch of beg ch-3. Fasten off.

Rnd 3: With RS facing, join 3rd color in any corner ch-3 sp, ch 3, *fptr around next dc, dc in same st as last fptr made, [fptr around next st, dc in next st] across, fptr around same st as last dc made**, (dc, ch 3, dc) in corner ch sp, rep from * around, ending last rep at **, dc in same ch sp as beg ch-3, ch 3, join in 3rd ch of beg ch-3. Fasten off.

Rnd 4: With 4th color, rep rnd 3. Fasten off. ■

GRANNY SQUARE 11

PATTERN NOTES

Uses 1 color.

Join with slip stitch as indicated unless otherwise stated.

Chain-3 at beginning of row or round counts as first double crochet unless otherwise stated.

INSTRUCTIONS
SQUARE

Rnd 1 (RS): Ch 4, sl st in first ch to form ring, **ch 3** (see Pattern Notes), 2 dc in ring, [ch 3 (corner), 3 dc in ring] 3 times, ch 1, join with dc in 3rd ch of beg ch-3, forming last corner ch sp.

Rnd 2: Ch 3, dc in same corner ch sp as beg ch-3, *dc dec (see Stitch Guide) in next 3 sts, ch 1**, (3 dc, ch 3, 2 dc) in corner ch sp, rep from * around, ending last rep at **, 3 dc in same ch sp as beg ch-3, ch 1, join with dc in 3rd ch of beg ch-3.

Rnd 3: Ch 3, dc in same corner ch sp as beg ch-3, *dc dec in next 3 sts, ch 1, 2 dc in next ch-1 sp, dc dec in next 3 sts, ch 1**, (3 dc, ch 3, 2 dc) in next corner ch sp, rep from * around, ending last rep at **, 3 dc in same ch sp as beg ch-3, ch 1, join with dc in 3rd ch of beg ch-3.

Rnd 4: Ch 3, dc in same corner ch sp as beg ch-3, *dc dec in next 3 sts, [ch 1, 2 dc in next ch-1 sp, dc dec in next 3 sts] twice, ch 1**, (3 dc, ch 3, 2 dc) in next corner ch-3 sp, rep from * around, ending last rep at **, 3 dc in same ch sp as beg ch-3, ch 3, **join** (see Pattern Notes) in 3rd ch of beg ch-3. Fasten off. ∎

GRANNY SQUARE 12

PATTERN NOTES
Uses 2 colors.

Join with slip stitch as indicated unless otherwise stated.

Chain-3 at beginning of row or round counts as first double crochet unless otherwise stated.

Chain-4 at beginning of row or round counts as first treble crochet unless otherwise stated.

INSTRUCTIONS
SQUARE
Rnd 1 (RS): With first color, ch 4, sl st in first ch to form ring, **ch 3** (see Pattern Notes), 11 dc in ring, **join** (see Pattern Notes) in 3rd ch of beg ch-3. Fasten off.

Rnd 2: With RS facing, join 2nd color in any st, ch 3, **fptr** (see Stitch Guide) around same st as beg ch-3, [dc in next st, fptr around same st as last dc worked] around, join in 3rd ch of beg ch-3. Fasten off.

Rnd 3: With RS facing, working in **back lps** (see Stitch Guide), join first color with sc in any st, sc in each st around, join in joining sc. Fasten off.

Rnd 4: With RS facing, join 2nd color with sc in any st above fptr in rnd 2, *fptr around post of fptr on rnd 2, sc in same st as last sc, ch 1, sk next st**, sc in next st, rep from * around, ending last rep at **, join in joining sc. Fasten off.

Rnd 5: With RS facing, join first color in any ch-1 sp, **ch 4** (see Pattern Notes), dtr in sk st on rnd 3, tr in same ch-1 sp on this rnd as beg ch-4, *ch 3 (corner), tr in same ch-1 sp as last tr, dtr in same sk st on rnd 3 as last dtr, tr in same ch-1 sp as last tr, [ch 1, dc in next ch-1 sp, tr in next sk st on rnd 3, dc in same ch-1 sp as last dc] twice, ch 1**, tr in next ch-1 sp, dtr in next sk st on rnd 3, tr in same ch sp as last tr, rep from * around, ending last rep at **, join in 4th ch of beg ch-4. Fasten off. ■

GRANNY SQUARE 13

PATTERN NOTES
Uses 2 colors.

Leave stitches behind post stitches unworked.

When working a stitch, a horizontal bar appears across back of stitch. When working in rounds, with only right side of stitch facing, this back horizontal bar cannot be seen. In order to find the bar, one must bend top 2 loops of stitch forward so that the bar, which was on the back, is now at the top and the two loops, which were on the top, are now at the front.

Join with slip stitch as indicated unless otherwise stated.

Chain-4 at beginning of row or round counts as first treble crochet unless otherwise stated.

Chain-3 at beginning of row or round counts as first double crochet unless otherwise stated.

INSTRUCTIONS
SQUARE
Rnd 1 (RS): With first color, ch 4, sl st in first ch to form ring, **ch 4** (see Pattern Notes), [3 dc in ring, tr in ring] 3 times, 3 dc in ring, **join** (see Pattern Notes) in 4th ch of beg ch-4.

Rnd 2: Ch 3 (see Pattern Notes), dc in same st as beg ch-3, *fptr (see Stitch Guide and Pattern Notes) around each of next 3 sts**, (2 dc, ch 3, 2 dc) in next st, rep from * around, ending last rep at **, 2 dc in same st as beg ch-3, ch 3, join in 3rd ch of beg ch-3. Fasten off.

Rnd 3: With RS facing, join 2nd color in **back horizontal bar** (see Pattern Notes) of 2nd fptr of fptr group, ch 4, *working in back horizontal bar of sts and in **back bar** (see illustration) of chs, tr in next st, dc in each of next 2 sts, hdc in next ch, sc in next ch, hdc in next ch, dc in each of next 2 sts, tr in next st**, (tr, ch 3, tr) in next st (corner), rep from * around, ending last rep at **, tr in same back horizontal bar as beg ch-4, ch 1, join with dc in 4th ch of beg ch-4, forming last ch sp.

Back Bar of Chain

Rnd 4: Ch 3, dc in same corner ch sp as beg ch-3, *dc in each of next 3 sts, fptr around each of next 5 sts, dc in each of next 3 sts**, (2 dc, ch 3, 2 dc) in corner ch-3 sp, rep from * around, ending last rep at **, 2 dc in same ch sp as beg ch-3, ch 3, join in 3rd ch of beg ch-3. Fasten off. ∎

GRANNY SQUARE 14

PATTERN NOTES
Uses 7 colors.

To make full-size afghan, repeat round 3 to desired size.

Join with slip stitch as indicated unless otherwise stated.

Chain-3 at beginning of row or round counts as first double crochet unless otherwise stated.

INSTRUCTIONS
SQUARE
Rnd 1 (RS): With first color, ch 4, sl st in first ch to form ring, **ch 3** (see Pattern Notes), dc in ring, [ch 3 (corner), dc around side of last dc made, 2 dc in ring] 3 times, ch 3, dc around side of last dc made, **join** (see Pattern Notes) in 3rd ch of beg ch-3. Fasten off.

Rnd 2: With RS facing, join 2nd color in any corner ch-3 sp, ch 3, *dc in each of next 3 sts, (2 dc, ch 3, dc around side of last dc made, dc) in next corner ch-3 sp, dc in each of next 3 dc*, (dc, **changing color**—see Stitch Guide to 3rd color, dc, ch 3, dc around side of last dc made, dc) in next corner ch-3 sp, rep between * once, 2 dc in same corner ch-3 sp as beg ch-3, ch 3, dc around side of last sc made, join in 3rd ch of beg ch-3. Fasten off both colors.

Rnd 3: With RS facing, join 4th color in last corner ch-3 sp on previous rnd, ch 3, *dc in each st across to next corner ch-3 sp, (2 dc, ch 3, dc around side of last dc, dc) in corner ch sp, dc in each st across*, (dc, changing to 5th color, dc, ch 3, dc around side of last dc made, dc) in next corner ch-3 sp, rep between * once, 2 dc in same corner ch sp as beg ch-3, ch 3, dc around side of last dc made, join in 3rd ch of beg ch-3. Fasten off both colors.

Rnd 4: Using 6th and 7th colors, rep rnd 3. ∎

GRANNY SQUARE 15

PATTERN NOTES

Uses 4 colors.

To make full-size afghan, repeat round 2 to desired size.

Join with slip stitch as indicated unless otherwise stated.

Chain-3 at beginning of row or round counts as first double crochet unless otherwise stated.

INSTRUCTIONS
SQUARE

Rnd 1 (RS): With first color, ch 4, sl st in first ch to form ring, **ch 3** (see Pattern Notes), 2 dc in ring, [ch 3 (corner), 3 dc in ring] 3 times, ch 3, **join** (see Pattern Notes) in 3rd ch of beg ch-3. Fasten off.

Rnd 2: With RS facing, join 2nd color in any corner ch-3 sp, ch 3, dc in same ch sp as beg ch-3, *dc in each st across to next corner ch-3 sp**, (2 dc, ch 3, 2 dc) in corner ch-3 sp, rep from * around, ending last rep at **, 2 dc in same ch sp as beg ch-3, ch 3, join in 3rd ch of beg ch-3. Fasten off.

Rnds 3 & 4: With rem colors, rep rnd 2. ∎

GRANNY SQUARE 16

PATTERN NOTES

Uses 2 colors.

Join with slip stitch as indicated unless otherwise stated.

Chain-3 at beginning of row or round counts as first double crochet unless otherwise stated.

INSTRUCTIONS
SQUARE

Rnd 1 (RS): With first color, ch 4, sl st in first ch to form ring, **ch 3** *(see Pattern Notes)*, 2 dc in ring, [ch 3 *(corner)*, 3 dc in ring] 3 times, ch 1, join with dc in 3rd ch of beg ch-3, forming last corner ch-3 sp. Fasten off.

Rnd 2: Ch 3, 2 dc in same corner ch sp as beg ch-3, *sk next dc, dc in next dc, sk next dc**, (3 dc, ch 3, 3 dc) in next corner ch-3 sp, rep from * around, ending last rep at **, 3 dc in same ch sp as beg ch-3, ch 2, join with sc in 3rd ch of beg ch-3, forming last corner ch sp.

Rnd 3: Ch 3, dc in same corner ch sp as beg ch-3, *dc in each of next 7 sts**, (2 dc, ch 3, 2 dc) in next corner ch-3 sp, rep from * around, ending last rep at **, 2 dc in same ch sp as beg ch-3, ch 3, **join** *(see Pattern Notes)* in 3rd ch of beg ch-3. Fasten off.

Rnd 4: With RS facing, join 2nd color in any corner ch-3 sp, ch 3, dc in same corner ch sp as beg ch-3, *dc in each of next 4 sts, **trtr** *(see Pattern Notes)* in sk st on rnd 1, dc in next st on this rnd, trtr in next sk st on rnd 1, dc in each of next 4 sts**, (2 dc, ch 3, 2 dc) in next corner ch-3 sp, rep from * around, ending last rep at **, 2 dc in same ch sp as beg ch-3, ch 3, join in 3rd ch of beg ch-3. Fasten off. ∎

GRANNY SQUARE 17

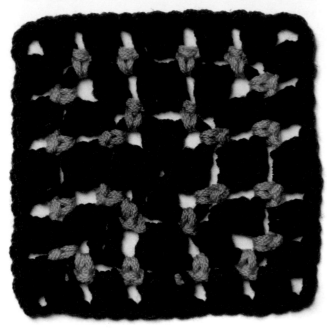

PATTERN NOTES

Uses 3 colors.

Join with slip stitch as indicated unless otherwise stated.

Chain-3 at beginning of row or round counts as first double crochet unless otherwise stated.

INSTRUCTIONS
SQUARE

Rnd 1 (RS): With first color, ch 4, sl st in first ch to form ring, **ch 3** *(see Pattern Notes)*, 2 dc in ring, [ch 3 *(corner)*, 3 dc in ring] 3 times, ch 3, **join** *(see Pattern Notes)* in 3rd ch of beg ch-3. Fasten off.

Rnd 2: With RS facing, join 2nd color with sc in any corner ch-3 sp, [ch 3, (sc, ch 3, sc) in next corner ch-3 sp] 3 times, ch 3, sc in same corner ch sp as joining sc, ch 3, join in joining sc. Fasten off.

Rnd 3: With RS facing, join first color in any corner ch-3 sp, ch 3, dc in same corner ch sp as beg ch-3, *ch 1, 3 dc in next ch-3 sp, ch 1**, (2 dc, ch 3, 2 dc) in next corner ch-3 sp, rep from * around, ending last rep at **, 2 dc in same corner ch sp as beg ch-3, ch 3, join in 3rd ch of beg ch-3. Fasten off.

Rnd 4: With RS facing, join 3rd color with sc in any corner ch-3 sp, *ch 2, sc in next ch-1 sp, ch 3, sc in next ch-1 sp, ch 2**, (sc, ch 3, sc) in next corner ch-3 sp, rep from * around, ending last rep at **, sc in same ch sp as joining sc, ch 3, join in joining sc. Fasten off.

Rnd 5: With RS facing, join first color in any corner ch-3 sp, ch 3, dc in same corner ch sp as beg ch-3, *ch 1, 2 dc in next ch-2 sp, ch 1, 3 dc in next ch-3 sp, ch 1, 2 dc in next ch-2 sp, ch 1**, (2 dc, ch 3, 2 dc) in next corner ch-3 sp, rep from * around, ending last rep at **, 2 dc in same corner ch sp as beg ch-3, ch 3, join in 3rd ch of beg ch-3. Fasten off. ■

GRANNY SQUARE 18

PATTERN NOTES
Uses 1 color.

Join with slip stitch as indicated unless otherwise stated.

Chain-3 at beginning of row or round counts as first double crochet unless otherwise stated.

INSTRUCTIONS
SQUARE
Rnd 1 (RS): Ch 4, sl st in first ch to form ring, **ch 3** (see Pattern Notes), 2 dc in ring, [ch 3 (corner), 3 dc in ring] 3 times, ch 1, join with dc in 3rd ch of beg ch-3, forming last corner ch sp.

Rnd 2: Ch 3, dc in same ch sp as beg ch-3, ***fptr** (see Stitch Guide) around each of next 3 sts**, (2 dc, ch 3, 2 dc) in next corner ch-3 sp, rep from * around, ending last rep at **, 2 dc in same ch sp as beg ch-3, ch 1, join with dc in 3rd ch of beg ch-3, forming last corner ch sp.

Rnd 3: Ch 3, dc in same ch sp as beg ch-3, *fptr around each of next 2 sts, **bptr** (see Stitch Guide) around each of next 3 sts, fptr around each of next 2 sts**, (2 dc, ch 3, 2 dc) in next corner ch sp, rep from * around, ending last rep at **, 2 dc in same ch sp as beg ch-3, ch 1, join with dc in 3rd ch of beg ch-3.

Rnd 4: Ch 3, dc in same ch sp as beg ch-3, *fptr around next st, bptr around each of next 3 sts, fptr around each of next 3 sts, bptr around each of next 3 sts, fptr around next st**, (2 dc, ch 3, 2 dc) in next corner ch-3 sp, rep from * around, ending last rep at **, 2 dc in same ch sp as beg ch-3, ch 3, **join** (see Pattern Notes) in 3rd ch of beg ch-3. Fasten off. ∎

GRANNY SQUARE 19

Chain-4 at beginning of row or round counts as first double crochet and chain-1 unless otherwise stated.

INSTRUCTIONS
SQUARE

Rnd 1 (RS): Ch 4, sl st in first ch to form ring, **ch 4** (*see Pattern Notes*), [dc in ring, ch 1] 7 times, **join** (*see Pattern Notes*) in 3rd ch of beg ch-4.

Rnd 2: Sl st in first ch-1 sp, *ch 9, sl st in next ch-1 sp, ch 4**, sl st in next ch-1 sp, rep from * around, ending last rep at **, join in first ch of beg ch-9.

Rnd 3: Sl st in first ch-9 sp, **ch 3** (*see Pattern Notes*), 2 dc in same ch sp as beg ch-3, *(ch 1, 3 dc, ch 3, 3 dc, ch 1, 3 dc) in same ch-9 sp, sl st in next ch-4 sp**, 3 dc in next ch-9 sp, rep from * around, ending last rep at **, join in 3rd ch of beg ch-3.

Rnd 4: Sl st in each of next 2 sts, sl st in next ch-1 sp, ch 3, 2 dc in same ch sp as beg ch-3, *ch 1, (3 dc, ch 3, 3 dc) in next corner ch sp, ch 1, 3 dc in next ch-1 sp, trtr in ch-4 sp on rnd 2**, 3 dc in next ch-1 sp, rep from * around, ending last rep at **, join in 3rd ch of beg ch-3. Fasten off. ∎

PATTERN NOTES
Uses 1 color.

Join with slip stitch as indicated unless otherwise stated.

Chain-3 at beginning of row or round counts as first double crochet unless otherwise stated.

GRANNY SQUARE 20

PATTERN NOTES
Uses 1 color.

For full-size afghan, repeat round 4 until afghan is desired size, ending each round with chain 1, join with double crochet in top of beg cluster until last round. At end of last round, ch 3, join with slip stitch in top of beg cluster. Fasten off

Join with slip stitch as indicated unless otherwise stated.

SPECIAL STITCHES
Beginning cluster (beg cl): Ch 2, holding back last lp of each st on hook, 2 dc as indicated in instructions, yo, pull through all lps on hook.

Cluster (cl): Holding back last lp of each st on hook, 3 dc as indicated in instructions, yo, pull through all lps on hook.

INSTRUCTIONS
SQUARE
Rnd 1 (RS): Ch 4, sl st in first ch to form ring, **beg cl** (*see Special Stitches*) in ring, [ch 3, **cl** (*see Special Stitches*) in ring, ch 3 (*corner*), cl in ring] 3 times, ch 3, cl in ring, ch 1, join with dc in top of beg cl, forming last corner ch sp. (*8 cl*)

Rnd 2: Beg cl in corner ch sp, [ch 2, dc in next ch-3 sp, ch 2, (cl, ch 3, cl) in next corner ch-3 sp] 3 times, ch 2, dc in next ch-3 sp, ch 2, cl in same ch sp as beg cl, ch 1, join with dc in top of beg cl, forming last corner ch sp.

Rnd 3: Beg cl in corner ch sp, *ch 2, 2 dc in next ch-2 sp, dc in next dc, 2 dc in next ch-2 sp, ch 2**, (cl, ch 3, cl) in next corner ch sp, rep from * around, ending last rep at **, cl in same ch sp as beg cl, ch 1, join with dc in top of beg cl, forming last corner ch sp.

Rnd 4: Beg cl in corner ch sp, *ch 2, 2 dc in next ch-2 sp, dc in each dc across to next ch-2 sp, 2 dc in ch-2 sp, ch 2**, (cl, ch 3, cl) in next corner ch-3 sp, rep from * around, ending last rep at **, cl in same ch sp as beg cl, ch 3, **join** (*see Pattern Notes*) in top of beg cl. Fasten off. ■

GRANNY SQUARE 21

PATTERN NOTES
Uses 1 color.

For full-size afghan, rep round 4 until afghan is desired size, ending each round with chain 1, join with double crochet in 3rd ch of beginning chain-3 until last round. At end of last round, ch 3, join with slip stitch in 3rd chain of beginning chain-3.

Join with slip stitch as indicated unless otherwise stated.

Chain-3 at beginning of row or round counts as first double crochet unless otherwise stated.

SPECIAL STITCH
Front post triple treble cross-st (fptrtr cross-st):
Fptrtr *(see Stitch Guide)* around post of post st 3 sts to left, (2 dc, ch 3, 2 dc) in next corner ch-3 sp, with hook in front of post st just made, fptrtr around post of post st 3 sts to right.

INSTRUCTIONS
SQUARE
Rnd 1 (RS): Ch 4, sl st in first ch to form ring, **ch 3** *(see Pattern Notes)*, 2 dc in ring, [ch 3 *(corner)*, 3 dc in ring] 3 times, ch 1, join with dc in 3rd ch of beg ch-3, forming last corner ch sp.

Rnd 2: Ch 3, dc in same ch sp as beg ch-3, *fptr *(see Stitch Guide)* around next st, sk st on this rnd behind fptr, dc in next st, fptr around next st, sk next st on this rnd behind fptr**, (2 dc, ch 3, 2 dc) in corner ch sp, rep from * around, ending last rep at **, 2 dc in same corner ch sp as beg ch-3, ch 1, join with dc in 3rd ch of beg ch-3.

Rnd 3: Ch 3, dc in same ch sp as beg ch-3, fptrtr around fptr 3 sts to right, *sk next dc, [dc in next dc, dc in next fptr] 2 times, dc in next dc, sk next dc**, **fptrtr cross st** *(see Special Stitch)*, rep from * around, ending last rep at **, with hook in back of first fptrtr made on this rnd, fptrtr around fptr 3 sts to left, 2 dc in same corner ch sp as beg ch-3, ch 1, join with dc in 3rd ch of beg ch-3.

Rnd 4: Ch 3, dc in same ch sp as beg ch-3, fptrtr around fptrtr 3 sts to right, *sk next dc, dc in each dc across to dc before next corner ch sp, sk next dc**, fptrtr cross-st, rep from * around, ending last rep at **, with hook in back of first fptrtr made on this rnd, fptrtr around fptrtr 3 sts to left, 2 dc in same corner ch sp as beg ch-3, ch 3, **join** *(see Pattern Notes)* in 3rd ch of beg ch-3. Fasten off. ■

GRANNY SQUARE 22

PATTERN NOTES
Uses 1 color.

Join with slip stitch as indicated unless otherwise stated.

Chain-3 at beginning of row or round counts as first double crochet unless otherwise stated.

SPECIAL STITCH
Cross-stitch (cross-st): Sk next 2 sts, **fpdtr** *(see Stitch Guide)* around next st, dc in first sk st, dc in next sk st, dc in same st as fpdtr, with hook in front of fpdtr just made, fpdtr around first sk st.

INSTRUCTIONS
SQUARE
Rnd 1 (RS): Ch 4, sl st in first ch to form ring, **ch 3** *(see Pattern Notes)*, 15 dc in ring, **join** *(see Pattern Notes)* in 3rd ch of beg ch-3. *(16 dc)*

Rnd 2: Ch 3, [**cross-st** *(see Special Stitch)*, (dc, ch 3, dc) in next st *(corner)*] 3 times, cross-st, dc in same st as beg ch-3, ch 1, join with dc in 3rd ch of beg ch-3, forming last corner ch sp.

Rnd 3: Ch 3, dc in same ch sp as beg ch-3, *dc in next st, **fptr** *(see Stitch Guide)* around next fpdtr, dc in each of next 3 sts, fpdtr around next fptr, dc in next st**, (2 dc, ch 3, 2 dc) in next corner ch sp, rep from * around, ending last rep at **, 2 dc in same corner ch sp as beg ch-3, ch 1, join with dc in 3rd ch of beg ch-3, forming last corner ch sp.

Rnd 4: Ch 3, dc in same corner ch sp as beg ch-3, *dc in each of next 3 dc, sk next fptr and next 3 dc, **fptrtr** *(see Stitch Guide)* around next fptr, dc in first sk dc, dc in each of next 2 sk dc, with hook in front of last fptrtr made, fptrtr around sk fptr, dc in each of next 3 dc**, (2 dc, ch 3, 2 dc) in next corner ch sp, rep from * around, ending last rep at **, 2 dc in same ch sp as beg ch-3, ch 3, join in 3rd ch of beg ch-3. Fasten off. ■

GRANNY SQUARE 23

PATTERN NOTES
Uses 1 color.

Join with slip stitch as indicated unless otherwise stated.

Chain-3 at beginning of row or round counts as first double crochet unless otherwise stated.

Chain-4 at beginning of row or round counts as first double crochet and chain-1 unless otherwise stated.

SPECIAL STITCH
Cluster (cl): Holding back last lp of each st on hook, 2 dc as indicated in instructions, yo, pull through all lps on hook

INSTRUCTIONS
SQUARE
Rnd 1 (RS): Ch 4, sl st in first ch to form ring, **ch 3** *(see Pattern Notes)*, **cl** *(see Special Stitch)* in ring, dc in ring, [ch 3 *(corner)*, (dc, cl, dc) in ring] 3 times, ch 1, join with dc in 3rd ch of beg ch-3, forming last corner ch sp.

Rnd 2: Ch 3, cl in same ch sp as beg ch-3, *dc in next dc, cl in next st, dc in next st**, (cl, dc, ch 3, dc cl) in next corner ch-3 sp, rep from * around, ending last rep at **, (cl, dc) in same ch sp as beg ch-3, ch 1, join with dc in 3rd ch of beg ch-3, forming last corner ch sp.

Rnd 3: Ch 3, cl in same ch sp as beg ch-3, *dc in next dc, cl in next st, dc in next st, ch 1, sk next st, dc in next st, cl in next st, dc in next st**, (cl, dc, ch 3, dc, cl) in next corner ch sp, rep from * around, ending last rep at **, (cl, dc) in same ch sp as beg ch-3, ch 1, join with dc in 3rd ch of beg ch-3.

Rnd 4: Ch 4 *(see Pattern Notes)*, *dc in next dc, cl in next st, dc in next st, [ch 1, sk next st or ch sp, dc in next st] 3 times, cl in next st, dc in next st, ch 1**, (dc, ch 3, dc) in corner ch sp, ch 1, rep from * around, ending last rep at **, dc in same ch sp as beg ch-3, ch 3, **join** *(see Pattern Notes)* in 3rd ch of beg ch-4. Fasten off. ∎

GRANNY SQUARE 24

PATTERN NOTES
Uses 1 color.

Join with slip stitch as indicated unless otherwise stated.

Chain-3 at beginning of row or round counts as first double crochet unless otherwise stated.

Chain-4 at beginning of row or round counts as first double crochet and chain-1 unless otherwise stated.

SPECIAL STITCH
Cluster (cl): Holding back last lp of each st on hook, 2 dc as indicated in instructions, yo, pull through all lps on hook.

INSTRUCTIONS
SQUARE
Rnd 1 (RS): Ch 4, sl st in first ch to form ring, **ch 3** *(see Pattern Notes)*, **cl** *(see Special Stitch)* in ring, dc in ring, [ch 3 *(corner)*, (dc, cl, dc) in ring] 3 times, ch 1, join with dc in 3rd ch of beg ch-3, forming last corner ch sp.

Rnd 2: Ch 3, cl in same ch sp as beg ch-3, *dc in next dc, cl in next st, dc in next st**, (cl, dc, ch 3, dc, cl) in next corner ch sp, rep from * around, ending last rep at **, (cl, dc) in same corner ch sp as beg ch-3, ch 1, join with dc in 3rd ch of beg ch-3, forming last corner ch sp.

Rnd 3: Ch 4 *(see Pattern Notes)*, *dc in first dc, ch 1, sk next st, dc in next st, cl in next st, dc in next st, ch 1, sk next st, dc in next st, ch 1**, (dc, ch 3, dc) in corner ch sp, ch 1, rep from * around, ending last rep at **, dc in same corner ch sp as beg ch-3, ch 1, dc in 3rd ch of beg ch-4, forming last ch sp.

Rnd 4: Ch 4, *dc in next dc, [ch 1, sk next ch or st, dc in next st] 5 times, ch 1**, (dc, ch 3, dc) in next corner ch-3 sp, ch 1, rep from * around, ending last rep at **, dc in same corner ch sp as beg ch-3, ch 3, **join** *(see Pattern Notes)* in 3rd ch of beg ch-4. Fasten off. ∎

GRANNY SQUARE 25

SPECIAL STITCH

Cluster (cl): Holding back last lp of each st on hook, 2 dc as indicated in instructions, yo, pull through all lps on hook.

INSTRUCTIONS
SQUARE

Rnd 1 (RS): Ch 4, sl st in first ch to form ring, **ch 4** (*see Pattern Notes*), [dc in ring, ch 3 (*corner*), dc in ring, ch 1] 3 times, dc in ring, ch 1, join with dc in 3rd ch of beg ch-4, forming last corner ch sp.

Rnd 2: **Ch 3** (*see Pattern Notes*), **cl** (*see Special Stitch*) in same ch sp as beg ch-3, *dc in next dc, cl in next ch-1 sp, dc in next st**, (cl, dc, ch 3, dc, cl) in next corner ch-3 sp, rep from * around, ending last rep at **, (cl, dc) in same corner ch sp as beg ch-3, ch 1, join with dc in 3rd ch of beg ch-3.

Rnd 3: Ch 4, *dc in next dc, [cl in next st, dc in next st] 3 times, ch 1**, (dc, ch 3, dc) in next corner ch-3 sp, ch 1, rep from * around, ending last rep at **, dc in same corner ch sp as beg ch-4, ch 1, join with dc in 3rd ch of beg ch-4.

Rnd 4: Ch 4, *dc in next dc, ch 1, sk next ch-1 sp, dc in next dc, [cl in next st, dc in next st] 3 times, ch 1, sk next ch-1 sp, dc in next dc, ch 1**, (dc, ch 3, dc) in next corner ch-3 sp, ch 1, rep from * around, ending last rep at **, dc in same corner ch sp as beg ch-4, ch 3, **join** (*see Pattern Notes*) in 3rd ch of beg ch-4. Fasten off. ∎

PATTERN NOTES

Uses 1 color.

Join with slip stitch as indicated unless otherwise stated.

Chain-3 at beginning of row or round counts as first double crochet unless otherwise stated.

Chain-4 at beginning of row or round counts as first double crochet and chain-1 unless otherwise stated.

GRANNY SQUARE 26

PATTERN NOTES
Uses 1 color.

Join with slip stitch as indicated unless otherwise stated.

Chain-3 at beginning of row or round counts as first double crochet unless otherwise stated.

INSTRUCTIONS
SQUARE
Rnd 1 (RS): Ch 4, sl st in first ch to form ring, **ch 3** (*see Pattern Notes*), 2 dc in ring, [ch 3 (*corner*), 3 dc in ring] 3 times, ch 1, join with dc in 3rd ch of beg ch-3, forming last corner ch sp.

Rnd 2: Ch 3, 2 dc in same corner ch sp as beg ch-3, [ch 1, (3 dc, ch 3, 3 dc) in next corner ch-3 sp] 3 times, ch 1, 3 dc in same corner ch sp as beg ch-3, ch 1, join with dc in 3rd ch of beg ch-3.

Rnd 3: Ch 3, 2 dc in same ch sp as beg ch-3, [ch 1, 3 dc in next ch-1 sp, ch 1, (3 dc, ch 3, 3 dc) in next corner ch-3 sp] 3 times, ch 1, 3 dc in next ch-1 sp, ch 1, 3 dc in same ch sp as beg ch-3, ch 1, join with dc in 3rd ch of beg ch-3.

Rnd 4: Ch 3, 2 dc in same ch sp as beg ch-3, *[ch 1, 3 dc in next ch-1 sp] twice, ch 1**, (3 dc, ch 3, 3 dc) in next corner ch-3 sp, rep from * around, ending last rep at **, 3 dc in same ch sp as beg ch-3, ch 3, **join** (*see Pattern Notes*) in 3rd ch of beg ch-3. Fasten off. ■

GRANNY SQUARE 29

PATTERN NOTES

Uses 2 colors.

Join with slip stitch as indicated unless otherwise stated.

Chain-3 at beginning of row or round counts as first double crochet unless otherwise stated.

INSTRUCTIONS
SQUARE

Rnd 1 (RS): With first color, ch 4, sl st in first ch to form ring, **ch 3** (see Pattern Notes), 2 dc in ring, [ch 3 (corner), 3 dc in ring] 3 times, ch 3 (corner), **join** (see Pattern Notes) in 3rd ch of beg ch-3. Fasten off.

Rnd 2: With RS facing, join 2nd color in any corner ch-3 sp, ch 3, 2 dc in same corner ch sp as beg ch-3, [ch 1, (3 dc, ch 3, 3 dc) in next corner ch sp] 3 times, ch 1, 3 dc in same corner ch sp as beg ch-3, ch 1, join with dc in 3rd ch of beg ch-3, forming last corner ch sp.

Rnd 3: Ch 3, 4 dc in same corner ch sp as beg ch-3, [sl st in next ch-1 sp, (5 dc, ch 3, 5 dc) in next corner ch-3 sp] 3 times, sl st in next ch-1 sp, 5 dc in same corner ch sp as beg ch-3, ch 3, join in 3rd ch of beg ch-3. Fasten off.

Rnd 4: With RS facing, join first color in any ch-3 sp, ch 3, 4 dc in same corner ch sp as beg ch-3, *working over sl st, 5 tr in ch-1 sp on rnd 2**, (5 dc, ch 3, 5 dc) in next corner ch sp, rep from * around, ending last rep at **, 5 dc in same corner ch sp as beg ch-3, ch 3, join in 3rd ch of beg ch-3. Fasten off. ■

GRANNY SQUARE 30

PATTERN NOTES
Uses 4 colors.

Join with slip stitch as indicated unless otherwise stated.

Chain-3 at beginning of row or round counts as first double crochet unless otherwise stated.

Chain-4 at beginning of row or round counts as first double crochet and chain-1 unless otherwise stated.

INSTRUCTIONS
SQUARE
Rnd 1 (RS): With first color, ch 4, sl st in first ch to form ring, **ch 3** *(see Pattern Notes)*, 2 dc in ring, [ch 3 *(corner)*, 3 dc in ring] 3 times, ch 3 *(corner)*, **join** *(see Pattern Notes)* in 3rd ch of beg ch-3. Fasten off.

Row 2: Now working in rows, with RS facing, join 2nd color in any ch-3 sp, ch 3, dc in same ch sp as beg ch-3, ch 1, (3 dc, ch 3, 3 dc) in next corner ch-3 sp, ch 1, 2 dc in next corner ch-3 sp, leaving rem sts unworked, turn.

Row 3 (WS): **Ch 4** *(see Pattern Notes)*, 3 dc in next ch-1 sp, ch 1, (3 dc, ch 3, 3 dc) in next corner ch sp, ch 1, 3 dc in next ch-1 sp, ch 1 *(corner)*, dc in last dc, leaving rem sts unworked, turn. Fasten off.

Row 4 (RS): Join 3rd color in corner ch-1 sp, ch 3, dc in same ch sp as beg ch-3, ch 1, 3 dc in next ch-1 sp, ch 1, (3 dc, ch 3, 3 dc) in next corner ch-3 sp, ch 1, 3 dc in next ch-1 sp, ch 1, 2 dc in last ch-1 sp, turn.

Row 5 (WS): Ch 4, [3 dc in next ch-1 sp, ch 1] twice, (3 dc, ch 3, 3 dc) in next ch-3 sp, ch 1, 3 dc in next ch-1 sp, ch 1, 3 dc in next ch-1 sp, ch 1 *(corner)*, dc in next dc, leaving beg ch-3 unworked, turn. Fasten off.

Rnd 6 (RS): Working around outer edge, join 4th color in unworked corner ch-3 sp on rnd 1, ch 3, 2 dc in same ch sp as beg ch-3, *[ch 1, 3 dc in next ch sp] twice, ch 1**, (3 dc, ch 3, 3 dc) in next corner ch sp, rep from * around, ending last rep at **, 3 dc in same corner ch sp as beg ch-3, ch 3, join in 3rd ch of beg ch-3. Fasten off. ■

GRANNY SQUARE 31

PATTERN NOTES
Uses 2 colors.

Join with slip stitch as indicated unless otherwise stated.

Chain-4 at beginning of row or round counts as first double crochet and chain-1 unless otherwise stated.

INSTRUCTIONS
SQUARE
Rnd 1 (RS): With first color, ch 4, sl st in first ch to form ring, **ch 4** (*see Pattern Notes*), [dc in ring, ch 3 (*corner*), dc in ring, ch 1] 3 times, dc in ring, ch 3, **join** (*see Pattern Notes*) in 3rd ch of beg ch-4. Fasten off.

Rnd 2: With RS facing, join 2nd color with sc in any corner ch-3 sp, *sc in next dc, working behind ch-1 sp, tr in ring on rnd 1 between next 2 dc, sc in next dc on this rnd**, (sc, ch 3, sc) in next corner ch-3 sp, rep from * around, ending last rep at **, sc in same corner ch sp as joining sc, ch 3, join in joining sc. Fasten off.

Rnd 3: With RS facing, join first color in any corner ch-3 sp, ch 4, *dc in next sc, [ch 1, sk next st, dc in next st] twice, ch 1**, (dc, ch 3, dc) in next corner ch-3 sp, ch 1, rep from * around, ending last rep at **, dc in same corner ch sp as beg ch-4, ch 3, join in 3rd ch of beg ch-4. Fasten off.

Rnd 4: With RS facing, join 2nd color with sc in any corner ch-3 sp, *sc in next dc, **working behind ch-1 sp, tr in corner ch-3 sp on rnd 2, sc in next dc on this rnd**, [working behind ch-1 sp, tr in sk st on rnd 2, sc in next dc on this rnd] twice, rep between ** once***, (sc, ch 3, sc) in next corner ch-3 sp, rep from * around, ending last rep at ***, sc in same corner ch sp as joining sc, ch 2, join with sc in joining sc, forming last corner ch sp.

Rnd 5: Ch 1, sc in corner ch sp just formed, *[ch 1, sk next st, sc in next st] 5 times, ch 1, sk next st**, (sc, ch 3, sc) in next corner ch-3 sp, rep from * around, ending last rep at **, sc in same corner ch sp as beg sc, ch 3, join in beg sc. Fasten off.

Rnd 6: All corner sts will be worked in corner ch-3 sps on rnd 4, encasing ch-3 corner of rnd 5 inside, with RS facing, join first color in any corner ch-3 sp of rnd 4, ch 3, *sc in next st on this rnd, [working in front of ch-1 sp, dc in sk st on rnd 4, sc in next st] 6 times**, (dc, ch 3, dc) in corner ch-3 sp on rnd 4, rep from * around, ending last rep at **, dc in same corner ch sp as beg ch-3, ch 3, join in 3rd ch of beg ch-3. Fasten off. ∎

GRANNY SQUARE 32

INSTRUCTIONS
SQUARE

Rnd 1 (RS): With first color, ch 4, sl st in first ch to form ring, **ch 3** (*see Pattern Notes*), 2 dc in ring, [ch 3 (*corner*), 3 dc in ring] 3 times, ch 3, **join** (*see Pattern Notes*) in 3rd ch of beg ch-3. Fasten off.

Rnd 2: With RS facing, join 2nd color in any corner ch-3 sp, ch 3, *fptr (*see Stitch Guide*) around 2nd dc on dc group, dc in each dc across same dc group, fptr around same 2nd dc on dc group as last fptr worked**, (dc, ch 3, dc) in next corner ch-3 sp, rep from * around, ending last rep at **, dc in same corner ch sp as beg ch-3, ch 3, join in 3rd ch of beg ch-3. Fasten off.

Rnd 3: With RS facing, join 3rd color in any corner ch-3 sp, ch 3, *sk next dc, fptr around next fptr, dc in dc just sk, dc in st behind fptr, dc in each of next 5 sts, fptr around fptr st 2 sts to right **, (dc, ch 3, dc) in next corner ch-3 sp, rep from * around, ending last rep at **, dc in same corner ch sp as beg ch-3, ch 3, join in 3rd ch of beg ch-3. Fasten off.

Rnd 4: With RS facing, join 4th color in any corner ch-3 sp, ch 3, dc in same ch sp as beg ch-3, *[dc in each of next 3 sts, **fptr dec** (*see Special Stitch*)] twice, dc in each of next 3 sts**, (2 dc, ch 3, 2 dc) in next corner ch-3 sp, rep from * around, ending last rep at **, 2 dc in same corner ch sp as beg ch-3, ch 3, join in 3rd ch of beg ch-3. Fasten off. ■

PATTERN NOTES
Uses 4 colors.

Join with slip stitch as indicated unless otherwise stated.

Chain-3 at beginning of row or round counts as first double crochet unless otherwise stated.

SPECIAL STITCH
Front post treble crochet decrease (fptr dec):
Holding back last lp of each st on hook, **fptr** (*see Stitch Guide*) around st 2 sts to right, fptr around st 2 sts to left, yo, pull through all lps on hook. Leave st behind fptr dec unworked.

GRANNY SQUARE 33

PATTERN NOTES
Uses 1 color.

Join with slip stitch as indicated unless otherwise stated.

Chain-3 at beginning of row or round counts as first double crochet unless otherwise stated.

Chain-6 at beginning of row or round counts as first double crochet and chain-3 unless otherwise stated.

Chain-5 at beginning of row or round counts as first double crochet and chain-2 unless otherwise stated.

INSTRUCTIONS
SQUARE
Rnd 1 (RS): Ch 4, sl st in first ch to form ring, **ch 3** (*see Pattern Notes*), 2 dc in ring, [ch 3 (*corner*), 3 dc in ring] 3 times, ch 1, join with dc in 3rd ch of beg ch-3, forming last corner ch sp.

Rnd 2: Ch 3, dc in same ch sp as beg ch-3, *dc in each of next 3 dc**, (2 dc, ch 3, 2 dc) in next corner ch-3 sp, rep from * around, ending last rep at **, 2 dc in same corner ch sp as beg ch-3, ch 1, join with dc in 3rd ch of beg ch-3.

Rnd 3: Ch 6 (*see Pattern Notes*), *dc dec (*see Stitch Guide*) in next 2 dc, dc dec in next 3 sts, dc dec in next 2 sts, ch 3**, (dc, ch 3, dc) in next corner ch-3 sp, ch 3, rep from * around, ending last rep at **, dc in same corner ch sp as beg ch-6, ch 1, join with dc in 3rd ch of beg ch-6, forming last corner ch sp.

Rnd 4: Ch 5 (*see Pattern Notes*), dc in same corner ch sp as beg ch-5, *ch 3, sk next ch-3 sp, dc dec in next 3 dc dec sts, ch 3, sk next ch-3 sp**, (dc, ch 2, dc, ch 3, dc, ch 2, dc) in next corner ch-3 sp, rep from * around, ending last rep at **, (dc, ch 2, dc) in same corner ch sp as beg ch-5, ch 3, **join** (*see Pattern Notes*) in 3rd ch of beg ch-5. Fasten off. ∎

GRANNY SQUARE 34

PATTERN NOTES
Uses 3 colors.

Work in continuous rounds; do not turn or join unless otherwise stated.

Mark first stitch of round.

Join with slip stitch as indicated unless otherwise stated.

Chain-3 at beginning of row or round counts as first double crochet unless otherwise stated.

INSTRUCTIONS
SQUARE
ZINNIA
BASE
Rnd 1 (RS): With flower color, ch 2, 6 sc in 2nd ch from hook, **do not join** (see Pattern Notes). (6 sc)

Rnd 2: Working in **back lps** (see Stitch Guide), 2 sc in each st around. (12 sc)

Rnd 3: Working in back lps, [2 sc in next st, sc in next st] around. (18 sc)

Rnd 4: Working in back lps, [2 sc in next st, sc in each of next 2 sts] around, **join** (see Pattern Notes) in back lp of next st. Fasten off.

BACKGROUND
Rnd 1: Join Background color in back lp of any st, [ch 2, sk next st, sl st in back lp of next st] 11 times, ch 2, sk next st and joining sl st, sl st in beg ch-2 sp. (12 ch-2 sps)

Rnd 2: Ch 4, (dc, hdc) in same ch sp as beg ch-4, *ch 1, 3 sc in next ch-2 sp, ch 1, (hdc, dc, tr) in next ch-2 sp**, ch 3 (corner), (tr, dc, hdc) in next ch-2 sp, rep from * around, ending last rep at **, ch 1, join with dc in 4th ch of beg ch-4, forming last ch sp.

Rnd 3: Ch 3 (see Pattern Notes), 2 dc in same corner ch sp as beg ch-3, *[ch 1, 3 dc in next ch-1 sp] twice, ch 1**, (3 dc, ch 3, 3 dc) in next corner ch-3 sp, rep from * around, ending last rep at **, 3 dc in same corner ch sp as beg ch-3, ch 3, join in 3rd ch of beg ch-3. Fasten off.

DISCS
Join center color in first front lp on rnd 1 of Base, (ch 3, sl st) in same st as last sl st, (sl st, ch 3, sl st) in each front lp around, join in joining sl st. Fasten off. (6 Discs)

RAYS
Join Ray color in next rem front lp on rnd 2, *ch 3, (dc, ch 2, sl st) in same st as beg ch-3**, sl st in each of next 2 front lps, rep from * around to last front lp on rnd 4 of Base, ending last rep at **, sl st in last front lp. Fasten off. (27 Rays) ∎

GRANNY SQUARE 35

PATTERN NOTES

Uses 1 color.

Join with slip stitch as indicated unless otherwise stated.

Chain-3 at beginning of row or round counts as first double crochet unless otherwise stated.

Leave st behind fptr unworked unless otherwise stated.

SPECIAL STITCH

Front post double treble crochet decrease (fpdtr dec): Holding back last lp of each st on hook, **fpdtr** (see Stitch Guide) around post st 3 sts to right, fpdtr around post st 1 st to left, yo, pull through all lps on hook.

INSTRUCTIONS
SQUARE

Rnd 1 (RS): Ch 4, sl st in first ch to form ring, **ch 3** (see Pattern Notes), 2 dc in ring, [ch 3 (corner), 3 dc in ring] 3 times, ch 2, join with sc in 3rd ch of beg ch-3, forming last corner ch sp.

Rnd 2: Ch 3, *fptr (see Stitch Guide) around first dc of next dc group, dc in same dc as fptr, dc in each of next 2 sts, fptr around last dc in same dc group**, (dc, ch 3, dc) in next corner ch sp, rep from * around, ending last rep at **, dc in same corner ch sp as beg ch-3, ch 2, join with sc in 3rd ch of beg ch-3.

Rnd 3: Ch 3, *fptr around next dc, dc in each of next 3 sts, **fpdtr dec** (see Special Stitch), working behind fpdtr dec, dc in same dc as last dc worked, dc in each of next 2 sts, fptr around last dc before corner**, (dc, ch 3, dc) in next corner ch-3 sp, rep from * around, ending last rep at **, dc in same corner ch sp as beg ch-3, ch 2, join with sc in 3rd ch of beg ch-3.

Rnd 4: Ch 3, *fptr around next dc, dc in same st as fptr worked around, [fptr around next st, dc in next st] 5 times, fptr around same st as last dc made**, (dc, ch 3, dc) in next corner ch-3 sp, rep from * around, ending last rep at **, dc in same corner ch sp as beg ch-3, ch 3, **join** (see Pattern Notes) in 3rd ch of beg ch-3. Fasten off. ∎

GRANNY SQUARE 36

PATTERN NOTES
Uses 2 colors.

Join with slip stitch as indicated unless otherwise stated.

Chain-3 at beginning of row or round counts as first double crochet unless otherwise stated.

Chain-4 at beginning of row or round counts as first treble crochet unless otherwise stated.

INSTRUCTIONS
SQUARE
Rnd 1 (RS): With first color, ch 4, sl st in first ch to form ring, **ch 3** (*see Pattern Notes*), 11 dc in ring, **join** (*see Pattern Notes*) in 3rd ch of beg ch-3. Fasten off. (*12 dc*)

Rnd 2: With RS facing, join 2nd color in any st, ch 3, **fptr** (*see Stitch Guide*) around same st as beg ch-3, [dc in next st, fptr around same st as last dc made] 11 times, join in **front lp** (*see Stitch Guide*) of 3rd ch of beg ch-3. (*24 sts*)

Rnd 3: Ch 1, sl st in same front lp as beg ch-1, [ch 1, sl st in front lp of next st] 23 times, join in beg ch-1. Fasten off.

Rnd 4: With WS facing, join first color in rem lp on rnd 2, **ch 4** (*see Pattern Notes*), working in rem lps of rnd 2, *2 dc in next st, **ch 1, hdc in each of next 3 sts, ch 1, 2 dc in next st*, (tr, ch 3, tr) in next st (*corner*), rep between * once***, tr in next st, **changing color** (*see Stitch Guide*) to 2nd color, **do not fasten off first color**, with 2nd color, ch 3, working over first color, tr in same st as last tr made, working over first color, 2 dc in next st, rep from ** around, ending last rep at ***, tr in same st as beg ch-4, ch 1, join with dc in 4th ch of beg ch-4, forming last corner ch sp, **turn.**

Rnd 5 (RS): Ch 3, 2 dc in same ch sp as beg ch-3, *ch 1, **[3 dc in next ch-1 sp, ch 1] twice*, (3 dc, ch 3, 3 dc) in next corner ch-3 sp, rep between * once***, bring first color up to ch-3 corner sp, (dc working over first color, dc not working over first color, dc changing to first color, ch 3, 3 dc) in ch-3 corner sp, ch 1, rep from ** around, ending last rep at ***, 3 dc in same corner ch sp as beg ch-3, ch 3, join in 3rd ch of beg ch-3. Fasten off both colors. ■

GRANNY SQUARE 37

PATTERN NOTES

Uses 1 color.

Join with slip stitch as indicated unless otherwise stated.

Chain-3 at beginning of row or round counts as first double crochet unless otherwise stated.

Chain-5 at beginning of row or round counts as first double crochet and chain-2 unless otherwise stated.

Chain-4 at beginning of row or round counts as first treble crochet unless otherwise stated.

SPECIAL STITCH

Front post double treble crochet decrease (fpdtr dec): Holding back last lp of each st on hook and working around post sts on rnd 2, **fpdtr** *(see Stitch Guide)* around post st to right and fpdtr around post st to left, yo, pull through all lps on hook.

INSTRUCTIONS
SQUARE

Rnd 1 (RS): Ch 4, sl st in first ch to form ring, **ch 5** *(see Pattern Notes)*, [dc in ring, ch 2] 7 times, **join** *(see Pattern Notes)* in 3rd ch of beg ch-5.

Rnd 2: Sl st in next ch-2 sp, **ch 3** *(see Pattern Notes)*, dc in same ch sp as beg ch-3, [ch 2, 2 dc in next ch-2 sp] 7 times, ch 2, join in 3rd ch of beg ch-3.

Rnd 3: Sl st in next st, sl st in next ch-2 sp, ch 1, sc in same ch sp as beg ch-1, * **fptr** *(see Stitch Guide)* around next dc on rnd 1, sc in same ch sp on this rnd as last sc made, ch 3, sk next 2 dc**, sc in next ch-2 sp, rep from * 7 times, ending last rep at **, join in joining sc..

Rnd 4: Sl st in each st across to first ch-3 sp, sl st in ch-3 sp, **ch 4** *(see Pattern Notes)*, 2 tr in same ch sp as beg ch-4, *ch 1, 3 dc in next ch-3 sp, ch 1**, (3 tr, ch 3, 3 tr) in next ch-3 sp *(corner)*, rep from * around, ending last rep at **, 3 tr in same ch sp as beg ch-4, ch 1, join with dc in 4th ch of beg ch-4, forming last corner ch sp.

Rnd 5: Ch 3, 2 dc in same corner ch sp as beg ch-3, *ch 1, 3 dc in next ch-1 sp, **fpdtr dec** *(see Special Stitch)*, 3 dc in next ch-1 sp, ch 1**, (3 dc, ch 3, 3 dc) in next corner ch-3 sp, rep from * around, ending last rep at **, 3 dc in same ch sp as beg ch-3, ch 3, join in 3rd ch of beg ch-3. Fasten off. ■

GRANNY SQUARE 38

PATTERN NOTES

Uses 1 color.

Join with slip stitch as indicated unless otherwise stated.

Chain-3 at beginning of row or round counts as first double crochet unless otherwise stated.

Chain-4 at beginning of row or round counts as first double crochet and chain-1 unless otherwise stated.

INSTRUCTIONS
SQUARE

Rnd 1 (RS): Ch 4, sl st in first ch to form ring, **ch 4** (see Pattern Notes), sl st in **back bar** (see illustration) of last ch made, [dc in ring, ch 1, sl st in back bar of last ch made] 7 times, **join** (see Pattern Notes) in 3rd ch of beg ch-4, drop lp from hook, pull dropped lp through st to back of work. (8 dc)

Back Bar of Chain

Rnd 2: Insert hook in dropped lp, ch 1, 2 **bpsc** (see Stitch Guide) around each dc around, join in beg bpsc.

Rnd 3: Ch 4, sl st in back bar of last ch made, dc in same st as beg ch-4, ch 1, sl st in back bar of last ch made, [dc, ch 1, sl st in back bar of last ch made] twice in each st around, join in 3rd ch of beg ch-4, drop lp from hook, pull dropped lp through st to back of work. (32 dc)

Rnd 4: Insert hook in dropped lp, ch 1, bpsc around each st around, join in beg bpsc.

Rnd 5: Ch 4, (tr, dc) in same st as beg ch-4, *ch 1, sk next 2 sts, (dc, hdc) in next st, (hdc, dc) in next st, ch 1, sk next 2 sts, (dc, 2 tr) in next st**, ch 3 (corner), (2 tr, dc) in next st, rep from * around, ending last rep at **, ch 1, join with dc in 4th ch of beg ch-4, forming last corner ch sp.

Rnd 6: Ch 3 (see Pattern Notes), 2 dc in same corner ch sp as beg ch-3, *[ch 1, 3 dc in next ch-1 sp] twice, ch 1**, (3 dc, ch 3, 3 dc) in next corner ch sp, rep from * around, ending last rep at **, 3 dc in same corner ch sp as beg ch-3, ch 3, join in 3rd ch of beg ch-3. Fasten off. ∎

GRANNY SQUARE 39

PATTERN NOTES

Uses 1 color.

Join with slip stitch as indicated unless otherwise stated.

Chain-3 at beginning of row or round counts as first double crochet unless otherwise stated.

Chain-4 at beginning of row or round counts as first double crochet and chain-1 unless otherwise stated.

INSTRUCTIONS
SQUARE

Rnd 1 (RS): Ch 4, sl st in first ch to form ring, **ch 4** *(see Pattern Notes)*, dc in ring, [ch 3 *(corner)*, (dc, ch 1, dc) in ring] 3 times, ch 2, join with sc in 3rd ch of beg ch-4, forming last corner ch sp.

Rnd 2: Ch 3 *(see Pattern Notes)*, dc in same corner ch sp as beg ch-3, *dc in next dc, ch 2, sk next ch-1 sp and next dc**, (dc, ch 3, 2 dc) in next corner ch-3 sp, rep from * around, ending last rep at **, dc in same corner ch sp as beg ch-3, ch 2, join with sc in 3rd ch of beg ch-3, forming last corner ch sp.

Rnd 3: Ch 3, dc in same corner ch sp as beg ch-3, *dc in each of next 3 dc, ch 2, dc in next ch-2 sp, ch 2**, (dc, ch 3, 2 dc) in next corner ch-3 sp, rep from * around, ending last rep at **, dc in same corner ch sp as beg ch-3, ch 2, join with sc in 3rd ch of beg ch-3, forming last corner ch sp.

Rnd 4: Ch 3, dc in same corner ch sp as beg ch-3, *dc in each of next 5 sts, [ch 2, dc in next ch-2 sp] twice ch 1**, (dc, ch 3, 2 dc) in next corner ch-3 sp, rep from * around, ending last rep at **, dc in same corner ch sp as beg ch-3, ch 3, **join** *(see Pattern Notes)* in 3rd ch of beg ch-3. Fasten off. ■

GRANNY SQUARE 40

Chain-4 at beginning of row or round counts as first double crochet and chain-1 unless otherwise stated.

INSTRUCTIONS
SQUARE

Rnd 1 (RS): Ch 4, sl st in first ch to form ring, **ch 4** *(see Pattern Notes)*, [dc in ring, ch 1] 7 times, **join** *(see Pattern Notes)* in 3rd ch of beg ch-4.

Rnd 2: Sl st in next ch-1 sp, *ch 7, sl st in next ch-1 sp, ch 5**, sl st in next ch-1 sp, rep from * around, ending last rep at **, join in beg sl st.

Rnd 3: Sl st in each of first 3 chs on beg ch-7, sl st in same ch-7 sp, *ch 7, sl st in same ch-7 sp as last sl st, ch 5, sl st in next ch-5 sp, ch 5**, sl st in next ch-7 sp, rep from * around, ending last rep at **, join in first sl st in first ch-7 sp.

Rnd 4: Sl st in each of first 3 chs of beg ch-7, sl st in same ch-7 sp, **ch 3** *(see Pattern Notes)*, 2 dc in same ch sp as beg ch-3, *[ch 1, 3 dc in next ch-5 sp] twice, ch 1**, (3 dc, ch 3, 3 dc) in next ch-7 sp *(corner)*, rep from * around, ending last rep at **, 3 dc in same ch-7 sp as beg ch-3, ch 3, join in 3rd ch of beg ch-3. Fasten off. ■

PATTERN NOTES
Uses 1 color.

Join with slip stitch as indicated unless otherwise stated.

Chain-3 at beginning of row or round counts as first double crochet unless otherwise stated.

GRANNY SQUARE 41

PATTERN NOTES
Uses 1 color.

Join with slip stitch as indicated unless
otherwise stated.

Chain-3 at beginning of row or round counts as
first double crochet unless otherwise stated.

Chain-4 at beginning of row or round counts as
first treble crochet unless otherwise stated.

SPECIAL STITCH
Double treble/3 (dtr/3): Yo 3 times, [insert hook in
next st, yo, pull lp through st] 3 times, yo, pull
through 4 lps on hook, [yo, pull through 2 lps
on hook] 3 times.

INSTRUCTIONS
SQUARE
Rnd 1 (RS): Ch 4, sl st in first ch to form ring,
ch 3 *(see Pattern Notes)*, 2 dc in ring, [ch 3
(corner), 3 dc in ring] 3 times, ch 1, join with dc
in 3rd ch of beg ch-3, forming last corner ch sp.

Rnd 2: **Ch 4** *(see Pattern Notes)*, (dc, hdc) in
same corner ch sp as beg ch-4, *sc in each of
next 3 sts**, (hdc, dc, tr, ch 3, tr, dc, hdc) in
next corner ch-3 sp, rep from * around, ending
last rep at **, (hdc, dc, tr) in same corner ch sp
as beg ch-4, ch 1, join with dc in 4th ch of beg
ch-4, forming last corner
ch sp.

Rnd 3: Ch 4, (dc, hdc) in same corner ch sp as
beg ch-4, *sc in next st, sl st in each of next 7 sts,
sc in next st**, (hdc, dc, tr, ch 3, tr, dc, hdc) in
next corner ch-3 sp, rep from * around, ending
last rep at **, (hdc, dc, tr) in same corner ch sp
as beg ch-4, ch 2, join with sc in 4th ch of beg
ch-4, forming last corner ch sp.

Rnd 4: Ch 1, sc in corner ch sp just formed, *hdc
in each of next 2 sts, dc in each of next 2 sts, tr
in each of next 2 sts, **dtr/3** *(see Special Stitch)*,
tr in each of next 2 sts, dc in each of next 2 sts,
hdc in each of next 2 sts**, (sc, ch 3, sc) in next
corner ch-3 sp, rep from * around, ending last
rep at **, sc in same corner ch sp as beg sc, ch 3,
join *(see Pattern Notes)* in beg sc. Fasten off. ∎

GRANNY SQUARE 42

PATTERN NOTES

Uses 1 color.

Join with slip stitch as indicated unless otherwise stated.

Chain-6 at beginning of row or round counts as first double crochet and chain-3 unless otherwise stated.

Chain-3 at beginning of row or round counts as first double crochet unless otherwise stated.

Chain-4 at beginning of row or round counts as first double crochet and chain-1 unless otherwise stated.

INSTRUCTIONS
SQUARE

Rnd 1 (RS): Ch 4, sl st in first ch to form ring, **ch 6** (*see Pattern Notes*), [2 dc in ring, ch 3] 3 times, dc in ring, **join** (*see Pattern Notes*) in 3rd ch of beg ch-6.

Rnd 2: Sl st in ch-3 sp, **ch 4** (*see Pattern Notes*), *working in front of ch-3 sp, dtr in ch-4 ring on rnd 1, ch 1, dc behind dtr in ch-3 sp on this rnd, ch 7**, dc in next ch-3 sp, ch 1, rep from * around, ending last rep at **, join in 3rd ch of beg ch-4.

Rnd 3: **Ch 3** (*see Pattern Notes*), *dtr in ch-3 sp on rnd 1, dc in next ch-1 sp on this rnd, **fptr** (*see Stitch Guide*) around next fpdtr, sk next st on this rnd behind fptr, dc in next ch-1 sp, dtr in ch-3 sp on rnd 1, dc in next st, ch 3 (*corner*), sk next ch-7 sp**, dc in next dc, rep from * around, ending last rep at **, join in 3rd ch of beg ch-3.

Rnd 4: Ch 3, *[fptr around next st, dc in next dc] 3 times, ch 1, working over ch-3 sp on rnd 3, (tr, ch 1, tr, ch 3, tr, ch 1, tr) in next ch-7 sp on rnd 2, ch 1**, dc in next dc, rep from * around, ending last rep at **, join in 3rd ch of beg ch-3. Fasten off. ■

GRANNY SQUARE 43

INSTRUCTIONS
SQUARE

Rnd 1 (RS): Ch 4, sl st in first ch to form ring, **ch 3** (*see Pattern Notes*), 2 dc in ring, [ch 3 (*corner*), 3 dc in ring] 3 times, ch 1, join with dc in 3rd ch of beg ch-3, forming last corner ch sp.

Rnd 2: Ch 3, 2 dc in same corner ch sp as beg ch-3, ch 1, (3 dc, ch 3, 3 dc) in next corner ch-3 sp, ch 1, (3 dc, ch 3, 2 dc) in next corner ch sp, dc in each of next 3 sts, (2 dc, ch 3, 2 dc) in next corner ch sp, dc in each of next 3 sts, 2 dc in same corner ch sp as beg ch-3, ch 1, join with dc in 3rd ch of beg ch-3, forming last corner ch sp.

Rnd 3: Ch 3, 2 dc in same corner ch sp as beg ch-3, ch 1, 3 dc in next ch-1 sp, ch 1, (3 dc, ch 3, 3 dc) in next corner ch-3 sp, ch 1, 3 dc in next ch-1 sp, ch 1, (3 dc, ch 3, 2 dc) in next corner ch-3 sp, dc in each st across to next corner ch sp, (2 dc, ch 3, 2 dc) in next corner ch-3 sp, dc in each st across to next corner ch sp, 2 dc in same corner ch sp as beg ch-3, ch 1, join with dc in 3rd ch of beg ch-3, forming last corner ch sp.

Rnd 4: Ch 3, 2 dc in same corner ch sp as beg ch-3, [ch 1, 3 dc in next ch-1 sp] twice, ch 1, (3 dc, ch 3, 3 dc) in next corner ch-3 sp, [ch 1, 3 dc in next ch-1 sp] twice, ch 1, (3 dc, ch 3, 2 dc) in next corner ch-3 sp, dc in each st across to next corner ch sp, (2 dc, ch 3, 2 dc) in next corner ch-3 sp, dc in each st across to next corner ch sp, 2 dc in same corner ch sp as beg ch-3, ch 3, **join** (*see Pattern Notes*) in 3rd ch of beg ch-3. Fasten off. ∎

PATTERN NOTES
Uses 1 color.

Join with slip stitch as indicated unless otherwise stated.

Chain-3 at beginning of row or round counts as first double crochet unless otherwise stated.

GRANNY SQUARE 44

PATTERN NOTES
Uses 3 colors.

Join with slip stitch as indicated unless otherwise stated.

Chain-3 at beginning of row or round counts as first double crochet unless otherwise stated.

Chain-4 at beginning of row or round counts as first treble crochet unless otherwise stated.

INSTRUCTIONS
SQUARE
MARIGOLD
DISCS
Rnd 1 (RS): With color for Ray, ch 2, 4 sc in 2nd ch from hook, **join** (see Pattern Notes) in beg sc. Fasten off. (4 sc)

Rnd 2: Join color for Disc in **front lp** (see Stitch Guide) of any st, ch 1, [sl st in front lp of next st, ch 1] 3 times, join in joining sl st. Fasten off.

RAYS
Rnd 1: With RS facing, working behind rnd 2 of Disc, join color for Ray in back lp of any st on rnd 1, [ch 2, sl st in back lp of next st on rnd 1] 3 times, ch 2, join in joining sl st.

Rnd 2: Ch 1, 3 sc in each ch-2 sp around, join in beg sc.

Rnd 3: Ch 3 (see Pattern Notes), dc in same st as beg ch-3, *(dc, ch 2, sl st) in next st**, (sl st, ch 3, dc) in next st, rep from * around, ending last rep at **, drop lp from hook, pull lp to back of work.

Rnd 4: Pick up dropped lp, working behind florets, [ch 3, sl st in back between next 2 florets] 5 times, ch 3, sl st in beg ch-3 sp.

Rnd 5: Ch 1, 4 sc in each ch-3 sp around, join in beg sc. (24 sc)

Rnd 6: Ch 4 (see Pattern Notes), tr in same st as beg ch-4, *tr in next st, (tr, ch 3, sl st) in next st**, (sl st, ch 4, tr) in next st, rep from * around, ending last rep at **, drop lp from hook, pull lp to back of work.

Rnd 7: Pick up dropped lp, working behind florets, [ch 4, sl st in back between next 2 florets] 7 times, ch 4, join in first ch of beg ch-4. Fasten off.

BACKGROUND
Rnd 1: Join Background color in any ch-4 sp, ch 4, (dc, hdc) in same ch sp as beg ch-4, *ch 1, 3 sc in next ch-4 sp, ch 1**, (hdc, dc, tr, ch 3, tr, dc, hdc) in next ch-4 sp, rep from * around, ending last rep at **, (hdc, dc, tr) in same ch sp as beg ch-4, ch 1, join with dc in 4th ch of beg ch-4, forming last corner ch sp.

Rnd 2: Ch 3, 2 dc in same corner ch sp, *[ch 1, 3 dc in next ch-1 sp] twice, ch 1**, (3 dc, ch 3, 3 dc) in next corner ch-3 sp, rep from * around, ending last rep at **, 3 dc in same corner ch sp as beg ch-3, ch 3, join in 3rd ch of beg ch-3. Fasten off.

EDGING

Join Disc color at base of any floret on rnd 3, *[ch 1, sl st in back lp of next st or ch on floret] around 1 floret, ending with sl st in back lp of last sl st on floret**, sl st in next sl st on next floret, rep from * around, ending last rep at **, join in joining sl st. Fasten off.

Rep on rnd 6. ■

GRANNY SQUARE 45

PATTERN NOTES

Uses 4 colors.

Join with slip stitch as indicated unless otherwise stated.

Chain-3 at beginning of row or round counts as first double crochet unless otherwise stated.

Chain-4 at beginning of row or round counts as first treble crochet unless otherwise stated.

Chain-5 at beginning of row or round counts as first double crochet and chain-2 unless otherwise stated.

INSTRUCTIONS
SQUARE
ASTER
PETALS

Rnd 1 (RS): With color for Petals, ch 2, 6 sc in 2nd ch from hook, **join** (see Pattern Notes) in beg sc. (6 sc)

Rnd 2: [Ch 7, working in **back bar** (see illustration) of chains, sc in 2nd ch from hook and in each ch across, sl st in same st as beg ch-7, sl st in next st] 6 times.

Back Bar of Chain

Rnd 3: *Sl st in back lp of each of next 7 chs, ch 2, sl st in back lp of each of next 6 sts**, sl st in back lp of each of next 2 sl sts, rep from * around, ending last rep at **, sl st in back lp of next sl st, drop lp from hook, pull lp to back of work.

Rnd 4: Pick up dropped lp, working behind petals, [ch 2, sl st in back between next 2 petals] 5 times, ch 2, sl st in first ch of beg ch-2. Fasten off.

BACKGROUND

Rnd 1: Join Background color in any ch-2 sp, **ch 5** (see Pattern Notes), dc in same ch sp as beg ch-5, [ch 2, (dc, ch 2, dc) in next ch-2 sp] 5 times, ch 2, join in 3rd ch of beg ch-5.

Rnd 2: Sl st in next ch-2 sp, **ch 4** (see Pattern Notes), (dc, hdc) in same ch sp as beg ch-4, *ch 1, (hdc, sc, hdc) in next ch-2 sp, ch 1, (hdc, dc, tr) in next ch-2 sp**, ch 3 (corner), (tr, dc, hdc) in next ch-2 sp, rep from * around, ending last rep at **, ch 1, join with dc in 4th ch of beg ch-4, forming last corner ch sp.

Rnd 3: Ch 3 (see Pattern Notes), 2 dc in same corner ch sp as beg ch 3, *[ch 1, 3 dc in next ch-1 sp] twice, ch 1**, (3 dc, ch 3, 3 dc) in next corner ch-3 sp, rep from * around, ending last rep at **, 3 dc in same corner ch sp as beg ch-3, ch 3, join in 3rd ch of beg ch-3. Fasten off.

DISCS
Rnd 1 (RS): With Disc color, ch 2, 6 sc in 2nd ch from hook, **do not join.** (6 sc)

Rnd 2: 2 sc in each st around, join in joining sc. Leaving long end for sewing, fasten off.

FINISHING
Using same color as Discs and another color, embroider **French knots** (see illustration) at random, covering rnds 1 and 2 of Discs.

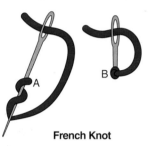

French Knot

Using long end, sew Discs to center of Petals. ■

GRANNY SQUARE 46

PATTERN NOTES
Uses 3 colors.

Join with slip stitch as indicated unless otherwise stated.

Chain-3 at beginning of row or round counts as first double crochet unless otherwise stated.

INSTRUCTIONS
SQUARE
DAISY
PETALS
Rnd 1 (RS): With color for Petals, ch 4, sl st in first ch to form ring, ch 1, [sc in ring, ch 1] 8 times, **join** (see Pattern Notes) in **front lp** (see Stitch Guide) of beg sc.

Rnd 2: [Ch 8, working in **back bar** (see illustration) of chain, sc in 2nd ch from hook and in each ch across, sl st in next ch-1 sp, ch 8, working in back bar, sc in 2nd ch from hook and in each ch across, sl st in front lp of next sc] 8 times. Fasten off.

Back Bar of Chain

BACKGROUND

Rnd 1: Push Petal toward center, working behind Petal, join color for Background with sc in any **back lp** (see Stitch Guide) of Petal on rnd 1, [ch 1, sc in back lp of next st] 7 times, ch 1, join in beg sc.

Rnd 2: Sl st in next ch-1 sp, **ch 3** (see Pattern Notes), 2 dc in same ch sp as beg ch-3, *ch 1, 3 dc in next ch-1 sp**, ch 3 (corner), 3 dc in next ch-1 sp, rep from * around, ending last rep at **, ch 1, join with dc in 3rd ch of beg ch-3, forming last corner ch sp.

Rnd 3: Ch 3, 2 dc in same ch sp as beg ch-3, *ch 1, 3 dc in next ch-1 sp, ch 1**, (3 dc, ch 3, 3 dc) in next corner ch sp, rep from * around, ending last rep at **, 3 dc in same corner ch sp as beg ch-3, ch 1, join with dc in 3rd ch of beg ch-3.

Rnd 4: Ch 3, 2 dc in same corner ch sp as beg ch-3, *[ch 1, 3 dc in next ch-1 sp] twice, ch 1**, (3 dc, ch 3, 3 dc) in next corner ch-3 sp, rep from * around, ending last rep at **, 3 dc in same corner ch sp as beg ch-3, ch 3, join in 3rd ch of beg ch-3. Fasten off.

DISCS

Rnd 1 (WS): With color for Discs, ch 2, 6 sc in 2nd ch from hook, **do not join**, mark first st of rnd. (6 sc)

Rnd 2: 2 sc in each st around, **do not join**. (12 sc)

Rnd 3: Sc in each st around, **do not join**.

Rnd 4: [Sc dec (see Stitch Guide) in next 2 sts] 6 times, join in next st. Leaving long end, fasten off.

Weave long end through top of sts on rnd 4, pull to close.

Sew Discs to center of Daisy. ∎

GRANNY SQUARE 47

PATTERN NOTES

Uses 2 colors.

Alternate colors throughout, work over dropped color where indicated.

Join with slip stitch as indicated unless otherwise stated.

Chain-3 at beginning of row or round counts as first double crochet unless otherwise stated.

INSTRUCTIONS
SQUARE

Rnd 1 (RS): Ch 4, sl st in first ch to form ring, **ch 3** (see Pattern Notes), 2 dc in ring, **changing color** (see Stitch Guide and Pattern Notes), dc in ring, dc in ring, changing color (see Stitch Guide and Pattern Notes) to 2nd color, [ch 3 (corner), working over dropped color, 2 dc in ring, dc in ring, changing color] twice, ch 3, working over dropped color, 3 dc in ring, ch 1, join with dc in 3rd ch of beg ch-3, forming last corner ch sp.

Rnd 2: Ch 3, 2 dc in same corner ch sp as beg ch-3, ch 1, bring dropped color up to next ch-3 corner, [(working over dropped color, 2 dc, dc, changing color, ch 3, working over dropped color, 3 dc) in corner ch-3 sp, ch 1] 3 times, working over dropped color, 3 dc in same corner ch sp as beg ch-3, ch 1, join with dc in 3rd ch of beg ch-3, forming last corner ch sp.

Rnd 3: Ch 3, 2 dc in same corner ch sp as beg ch-3, ch 1, bring dropped color up to next ch-1 sp, *working over dropped color, 3 dc in next ch-1 sp, ch 1**, (working over dropped color, 2 dc, dc, changing color, ch 3, working over dropped color, 3 dc) in next corner ch-3 sp, ch 1, rep from * around, ending last rep at **, working over dropped color, 3 dc in same corner ch sp as beg ch-3, ch 1, join with dc in 3rd ch of beg ch-3, forming last corner ch sp.

Rnd 4: Ch 3, 2 dc in same corner ch sp as beg ch-3, ch 1, bring dropped color up to next ch-1 sp, *[working over dropped color, 3 dc in next ch-1 sp, ch 1] twice**, (working over dropped color, 2 dc, dc, changing color, ch 3, working over dropped color, 3 dc) in next corner ch-3 sp, ch 1, rep from * around, ending last rep at **, 3 dc in same corner ch sp as beg ch-3, ch 3, **join** *(see Pattern Notes)* in 3rd ch of beg ch-3. Fasten off both colors. ■

GRANNY SQUARE 48

PATTERN NOTES
Uses 3 colors.

Join with slip stitch as indicated unless otherwise stated.

Chain-4 at beginning of row or round counts as first treble crochet unless otherwise stated.

INSTRUCTIONS
SQUARE
STAR
Rnd 1 (RS): With Star color, ch 4, sl st in first ch to form ring, ch 1, 10 sc in ring, **join** *(see Pattern Notes)* in beg sc.

Rnd 2: Ch 3, tr in next st (ch-3 and tr counts as beg tr dec), [ch 5, **tr dec** *(see Stitch Guide)* in next 2 sts] 4 times, ch 5, join in top of beg tr dec. Fasten off.

RING
Rnd 1: With RS facing, join ring color with sc in any ch-5 sp, 7 sc in same ch sp as joining sc, 7 sc in each ch sp around, join in joining sc. *(36 sc)*

Rnd 2: Ch 1, sc in first st, [ch 3, sk next 2 sts, sc in next st] 11 times, ch 3, sk next 2 sts, join in beg sc. Fasten off.

BACKGROUND
With RS facing, join Background color in any ch-3 sp, **ch 4** *(see Pattern Notes)*, 2 tr in same ch sp as beg ch-4, *[ch 1, 3 dc in next ch-3 sp] twice, ch 1**, (3 tr, ch 3, 3 tr) in next ch sp *(corner)*, rep from * around, ending last rep at **, 3 tr in same ch sp as beg ch-4, ch 3, join in 4th ch of beg ch-4. Fasten off. ■

GRANNY SQUARE 49

INSTRUCTIONS
SQUARE

Rnd 1 (RS): With first color, ch 4, sl st in first ch to form ring, **ch 3** *(see Pattern Notes)*, **fpdc** *(see Stitch Guide) (beg Y-st)*, [ch 1, **Y-st** *(see Special Stitch)* in ring] 7 times, ch 1, **join** *(see Pattern Notes)* in 3rd ch of beg ch-3. Fasten off.

Rnd 2: With RS facing, join 2nd color in any ch-1 sp, ch 3, fpdc around beg ch-3, ch 3 *(corner)*, Y-st in same ch sp as beg ch-3, *ch 1, Y-st in next ch-1 sp, ch 1**, (Y-st, ch 3, Y-st) in next ch-1 sp *(corner)*, rep from * around, ending last rep at **, join in 3rd ch of beg ch-3. Fasten off.

Rnd 3: With RS facing, join 3rd color in any corner ch-3 sp, ch 3, fpdc around beg ch-3, ch 3 *(corner)*, Y-st in same ch sp as beg ch-3, *ch 1, [Y-st in next ch-3 sp, ch 1] twice**, (Y-st, ch 3, Y-st) in next corner ch-3 sp *(corner)*, rep from * around, ending last rep at **, join in 3rd ch of beg ch-3. Fasten off.

Rnd 4: With RS facing, join 4th color in any corner ch-3 sp, ch 3, fpdc around beg ch-3, ch 3 *(corner)*, Y-st in same ch sp as beg ch-3, *ch 1, Y-st in next ch-1 sp, ch 1, dc in next ch-1 sp, fpdc around last dc made, **fptr** *(see Stitch Guide)* around same dc as last fpdc made, ch 1, Y-st in next ch-1 sp, ch 1**, (Y-st, ch 3, Y-st) in next corner ch-3 sp, rep from * around, ending last rep at **, join in 3rd ch of beg ch-3. Fasten off. ∎

PATTERN NOTES
Uses 4 colors.

Join with slip stitch as indicated unless otherwise stated.

Chain-3 at beginning of row or round counts as first double crochet unless otherwise stated.

SPECIAL STITCH
Y-stitch (Y-st): Dc as indicated in instructions, fpdc around post of dc just made.

GRANNY SQUARE 50

Chain-5 at beginning of row or round counts as first triple treble crochet unless otherwise stated.

Chain-4 at beginning of row or round counts as first treble crochet unless otherwise stated.

INSTRUCTIONS
SQUARE
Rnd 1 (RS): Ch 4, sl st in first ch to form ring, **ch 5** (*see Pattern Notes*), 27 trtr in ring, **join** (*see Pattern Notes*) in 5th ch of beg ch-5. (*28 trtr*)

Rnd 2: Ch 4 (*see Pattern Notes*), tr in same st as beg ch-4, *dc in next st, 2 hdc in next st, sc in next st, 2 hdc in next st, dc in next st, 2 tr in next st**, ch 3 (*corner*), 2 tr in next st, rep from * around, ending last rep at **, ch 1, join with dc in 4th ch of beg ch-4, forming last corner ch sp.

Rnd 3: Ch 1, 2 sc in same corner ch sp as beg ch-1, *sc in each of next 11 sts**, (2 sc, ch 3, 2 sc) in next corner ch sp, rep from * around, ending last rep at **, 2 sc in same corner ch sp as beg ch-1, ch 3, join in beg sc. Fasten off. ∎

PATTERN NOTES
Uses 1 color.

Join with slip stitch as indicated unless otherwise stated.

Filet
Instructions

CHARTS

When following Chart while working back and forth rows:

A. Odd-numbered rows are worked from right to left;

B. Even-numbered rows are worked from left to right.

When following Chart while working in rnds, all rnds are worked from right to left.

SPECIAL STITCH

Cluster (cl): Holding back last lp of each st on hook, 2 dc as indicated in instructions or on Chart, yo, pull through all lps on hook.

BASIC FILET STITCHES

Beginning open block (beg open block): Ch 4 *(counts as first dc and ch-1)*, sk first st or ch, dc in next st.

Open block: Ch 1, sk next st or ch, dc in next st.

Beginning solid block (beg solid block): Ch 3 *(counts as first dc)*, **cl** *(see Special Stitch)* in next st or ch, dc in next st.

Solid block: Cl in next st or ch, dc in next st.

Beginning lacet (beg lacet): Ch 5 *(counts as dc and ch-2)*, sk next st or ch, sl st in next st or ch, ch 2, sk next st or ch, dc in next st.

Lacet: Ch 2, sk next st or ch, sl st in next st or ch, ch 2, sk next st or ch, dc in next st.

Double open block: Ch 3, sk next 3 sts or chs, dc in next st.

End open half block: When working last dc of solid or open block right before half open block, dc in st until 2 lps rem on hook, sk next st or ch, yo, insert hook in next st, yo, pull through st, yo, pull through 2 lps on hook, yo, pull through all lps on hook.

Beginning open half block (beg open half block): Ch 2, sk next st or ch, dc in next st.

Attaching beginning open block (attaching beg open block): Join in crochet piece, ch 4 *(counts as dc and ch-1)*, dc in crochet piece.

Attaching open block: Ch 1, dc in crochet piece.

Joining open block: Ch 1, join in 3rd ch of beg ch.

Joining solid block: Cl in next st or ch, join with sl st in 3rd ch of beg ch.

Joining lacet: Ch 2, sk next st or ch, sl st in next st or ch, ch 2, sk next st or ch, join in 3rd ch of beg ch.

INCREASING & DECREASING IN FILET

Beginning solid block increase (beg solid block inc): Ch 4, cl in 4th ch from hook, dc in next dc.

Beginning open block increase (beg open block inc): Ch 5, sk chs, dc in next dc.

End solid block increase (end solid block inc): Yo, insert hook in same st as last dc made, yo, pull lp through, yo, pull through 1 lp on hook (*this forms base of first st*), yo, pull through 2 lps on hook, yo, insert hook in base of st just made, yo, pull lp through, yo, pull through 2 lps on hook, yo, pull through all lps on hook, yo, insert hook in base of last st, yo, pull lp through, yo, pull through 1 lp on hook (*forms base of 2nd st*), [yo, pull through 2 lps on hook] twice.

End open block increase (end open block inc): Ch 1, tr in same st as last dc made.

Beginning decrease (beg dec): Sl st across number of sts to be decreased, sl st in next dc, ch 3 to beg next row.

End decrease (end dec): Work according to chart across, leaving number of sts to be decreased unworked.

First stitch (first st): If next row doesn't beg with inc or dec, ch 3 to beg row.

CREATE YOUR OWN FILET DESIGN

Blank charts of each type are provided in each section. Using pencil, place an X on each square that you would like to be a solid block to create your own unique design. ■

FILET SMALL SQUARES

PATTERN NOTE
See Filet Instructions on pages 54 and 55.

SPECIAL STITCH
See Special Stitch and Basic Filet Stitches on page 54.

INSTRUCTIONS
Row 1: Ch 18, dc in 6th ch from hook for first open block, work according to row 1 on chart of your choice, using Special Stitches as needed.

Next rows: Work according to chart. At end of last row, fasten off. ■

STITCH KEY
- ☐ First open block
- ● Beginning open block
- ☐ Open block
- ☒ Solid block

Blank Chart

Chart A

Chart B

Chart C

Chart D

Chart E

Chart F

Chart G

Chart H

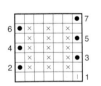

Chart I

Chart J

Chart K

Chart L

Chart M

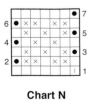

Chart N

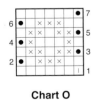

Chart O

Chart P

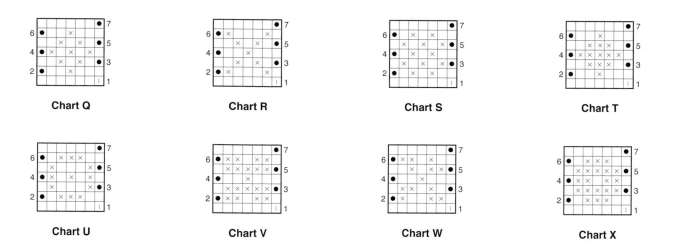

| Chart Q | Chart R | Chart S | Chart T |
| Chart U | Chart V | Chart W | Chart X |

FILET LARGE SQUARES

PATTERN NOTE

See Filet Instructions on pages 54 and 55.

SPECIAL STITCH

See Special Stitch and Basic Filet Stitches on page 54.

INSTRUCTIONS

Row 1: Ch 38, dc in 6th ch from hook for first open block, work according to row 1 on chart of your choice, using Special Stitches as needed.

Next rows: Work according to chart. At end of last row, fasten off. ∎

STITCH KEY
- ⊡ First open block
- ⊙ Beginning open block
- ☐ Open block
- ⊠ Solid block

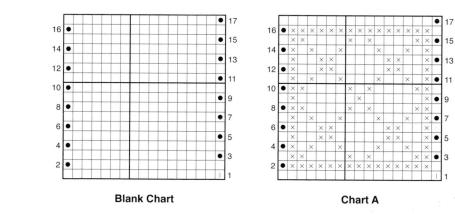

Blank Chart   Chart A

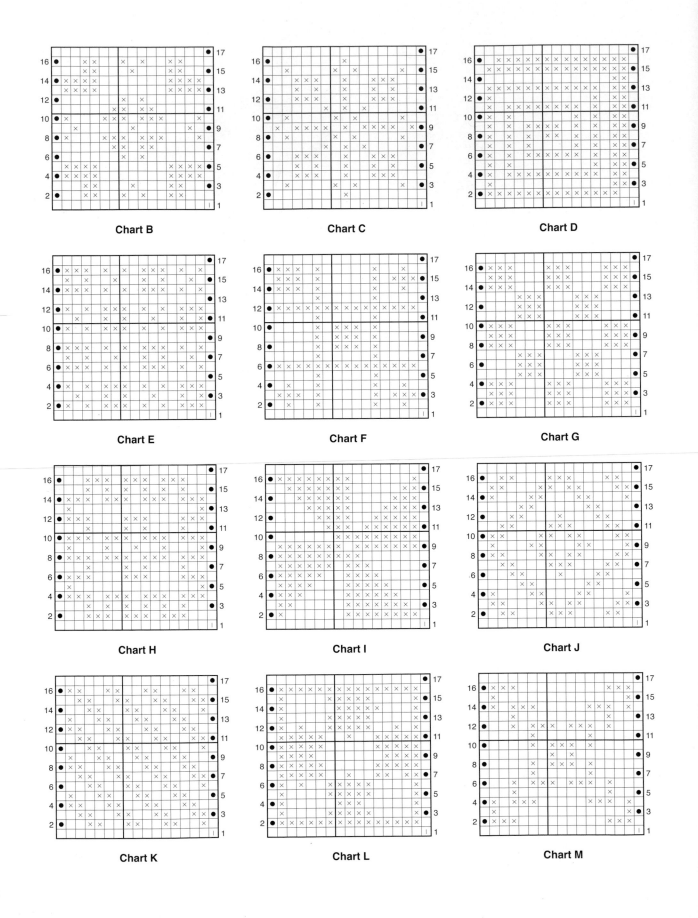

Chart B

Chart C

Chart D

Chart E

Chart F

Chart G

Chart H

Chart I

Chart J

Chart K

Chart L

Chart M

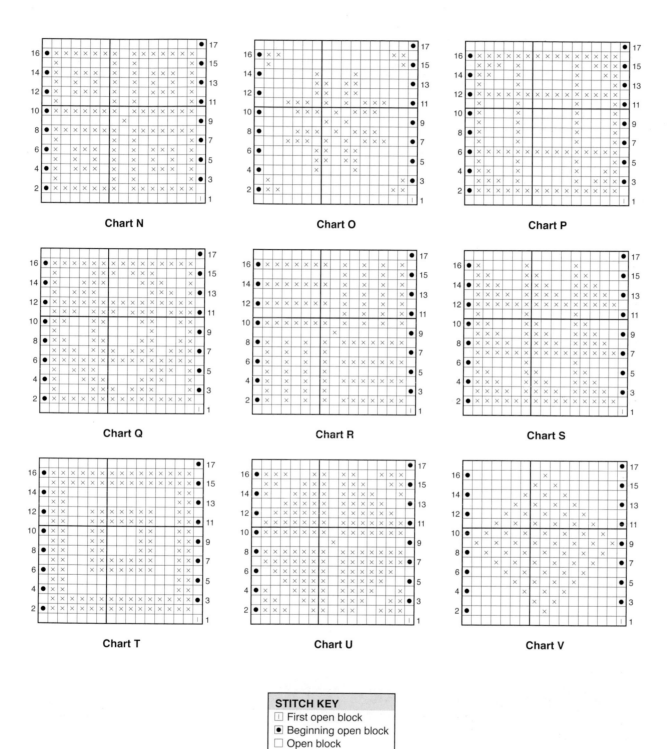

Chart N

Chart O

Chart P

Chart Q

Chart R

Chart S

Chart T

Chart U

Chart V

STITCH KEY
⊟ First open block
⊡ Beginning open block
☐ Open block
☒ Solid block

FILET HALF SQUARES

PATTERN NOTE
See Filet Instructions on pages 54 and 55.

SPECIAL STITCH
See Special Stitch and Basic Filet Stitches on page 54.

INSTRUCTIONS
Row 1: Ch 18, dc in 6th ch from hook for first open block, work according to row 1 on chart of your choice, using Special Stitches as needed.

Next rows: Work according to chart. At end of last row, fasten off. ∎

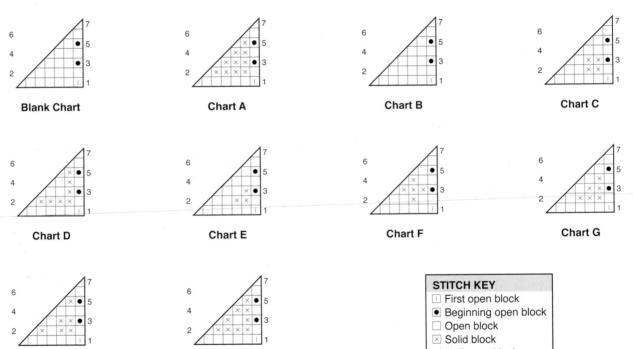

Blank Chart   Chart A   Chart B   Chart C

Chart D   Chart E   Chart F   Chart G

Chart H   Chart I

STITCH KEY
☐ First open block
⬤ Beginning open block
☐ Open block
☒ Solid block
◿ Half open block

FILET RECTANGLE

PATTERN NOTE
See Filet Instructions on pages 54 and 55.

SPECIAL STITCH
See Special Stitch and Basic Filet Stitches on page 54.

INSTRUCTIONS
Row 1: Ch 22, dc in 6th ch from hook for first open block, work according to row 1 on chart of your choice, using Special Stitches as needed.

Next rows: Work according to chart. At end of last row, fasten off. ∎

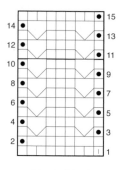

Blank Chart

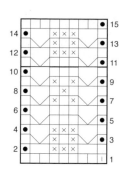

Chart A

Chart B

Chart C

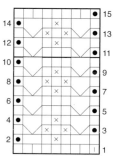

Chart D

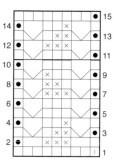

Chart E

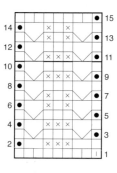

Chart F

Chart G

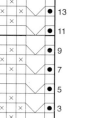

Chart H

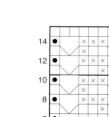

Chart I

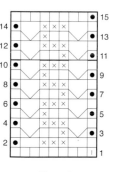

Chart J

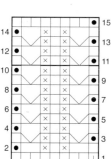
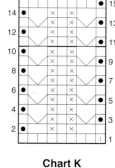

Chart K

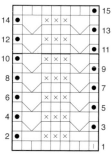

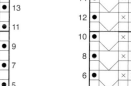

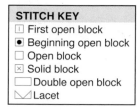

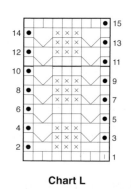

Chart L

STITCH KEY
- ⊡ First open block
- ● Beginning open block
- ☐ Open block
- ⊠ Solid block
- ▭ Double open block
- ◹ Lacet

FILET FRINGE

PATTERN NOTE
See Filet Instructions on pages 54 and 55.

SPECIAL STITCH
See Special Stitch and Basic Filet Stitches
on page 54.

INSTRUCTIONS
Row 1: Join in first st on design, work as follows:

A. if row 1 is solid block work, ch 4, cl in 4th ch
from hook, sk next st on design, sl st in next
st on design, ch 1, sk next st, sl st in next st on
design, turn;

B. if row 1 is open block work, ch 5, sk next st
on design, sl st in next st on design, ch 1, sk
next st, sl st in next st on design, turn.

Next rows: Continue attaching to design, if at
design edge at end of row, omit last dc on open
or solid block, sk next st on design, sl st in next
st, ch 1, sk next st on design, sl st in next st,
turn. At end of last row, fasten off. ■

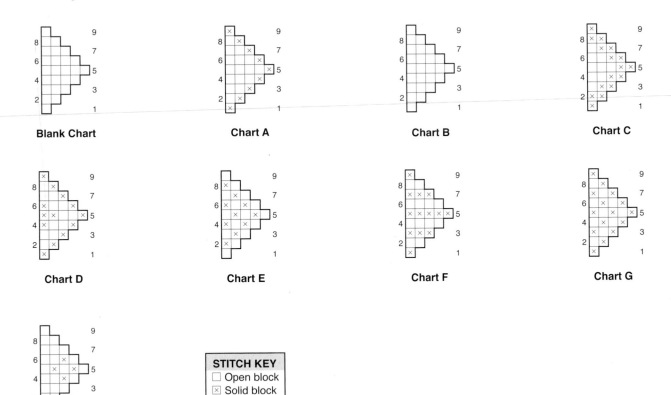

Blank Chart Chart A Chart B Chart C

Chart D Chart E Chart F Chart G

Chart H

STITCH KEY
☐ Open block
☒ Solid block

FILET IN THE ROUND 1

PATTERN NOTE
See Filet Instructions on pages 54 and 55.

SPECIAL STITCH
See Special Stitch and Basic Filet Stitches on page 54.

INSTRUCTIONS
Rnd 1: Beg open block *(see Basic Filet Stitches on page 54)*, work according to chart of choice, using Special Stitches as needed.

Next rnds: Work according to chart. At end of last rnd, fasten off. ■

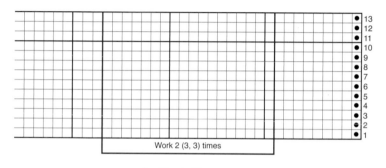

Blank Chart

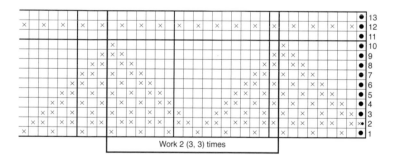

Chart A

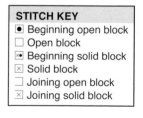

STITCH KEY
- ⊡ Beginning open block
- ☐ Open block
- ⊠ Beginning solid block
- ⊠ Solid block
- ⊐ Joining open block
- ⊠ Joining solid block

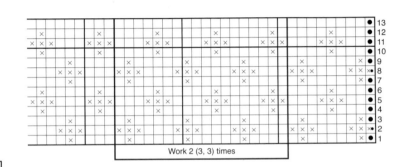

Chart B

Chart C

STITCH KEY
- ⊡ Beginning open block
- ☐ Open block
- ⊠ Beginning solid block
- ☒ Solid block
- ☐ Joining open block
- ☒ Joining solid block

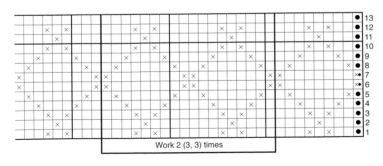

Chart D

Chart E

FILET IN THE ROUND 2

PATTERN NOTE
See Filet Instructions on pages 54 and 55.

SPECIAL STITCH
See Special Stitch and Basic Filet Stitches on page 54.

INSTRUCTIONS
Rnd 1: Evenly sp **attaching beg open block** (*see Basic Filet Stitches on page 54*), 28 **attaching open block** (*see Basic Filet Stitches on page 54*), **joining open block** (*see Basic Filet Stitches on page 54*).

Next rnds: Work according to chart. At end of last rnd, fasten off. ■

Blank Chart

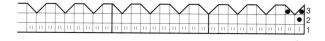

Chart A

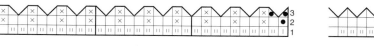

Chart B

Chart C

Chart D

Chart E

Chart F

Chart G

Chart H

Chart I

STITCH KEY
- ⊡ Attaching beg open block
- ⊞ Attaching open block
- ⊡ Beginning open block
- ☐ Open block
- ⊠ Beginning solid block
- ⊠ Solid block
- ◣ Beg lacet
- ⋁ Lacet
- ⊡ Joining open block
- ⊠ Joining solid block
- ⋁ Joining lacet

Pillow

SKILL LEVEL

INTERMEDIATE

FINISHED SIZE

12 inches square

MATERIALS

- Berroco Comfort DK light (DK) weight yarn (1¾ oz/178 yds/ 50g per ball):
  300 yds various colors of yarn for 18 granny and filet pieces chosen
- Size F/5/3.75mm crochet hook or size needed to obtain gauge
- Tapestry needle
- 12" square pillow form with black cover

GAUGE

Granny Squares = 3¾ inches square

PATTERN NOTE

Will be listed with each Square as needed.

SPECIAL STITCHES

Will be listed with each Square as needed.

INSTRUCTIONS

PILLOW

Make a total of 18 Squares from the Granny Square Collection and Filet Small Square Collection.

Add Edging to Filet Squares only.

FILET SQUARE EDGING

With RS facing, join with sc in top right corner open block, sc in same open block as joining sc, *[sc in next st, sc in next open block] 5 times, sc in next st**, (2 sc, ch 3, 2 sc) in corner open block, rep from * around, ending last rep at **, 2 sc in same corner open block as joining sc, ch 3, join with sl st in joining sc. Fasten off.

ASSEMBLY

Arrange 18 Squares to form two 3-Square x 3-Square pieces. Using Sewing Method, sew Squares in each column tog, forming 3 columns of 3 Squares, then sew columns tog.

SEWING METHOD
SEW SQUARES TOGETHER

Place 2 Squares tog with RS facing, using only outer lps of sts and chs, whipstitch pieces tog along 1 side starting with outer lp of 2nd ch in first ch-3 corner and ending outer lp of 2nd ch in last ch-3 corner.

SEW COLUMNS TOGETHER

Sew columns tog using same method as Sew Squares Together. When sewing where 2 Squares are joined, working ch-3 corners of current Squares, work whipstitch through outer lp of first ch, whipstitch through outer lp of 2nd ch, then working in ch-3 corners of next Squares, whipstitch through outer lp of 2nd ch, whipstitch through outer lp of 3rd ch.

FINISHING

Rnd 1: Place two assembled pieces WS tog with pillow form in between, working in inner lps through both thicknesses, join with sc, evenly sp sc around with ch 1 at each corner, join with sl st in beg sc.

Rnd 2: Ch 1, working from left to right, **reverse sc** *(see Stitch Guide)* in each st and ch around, join with sl st in beg reverse sc. Fasten off. ■

Scarf

SKILL LEVEL
INTERMEDIATE

FINISHED SIZE
65 inches

MATERIALS
- Berroco Comfort DK light (DK) weight yarn (1¾ oz/178 yds/ 50g per ball):
  400 yds various colors of yarn for 6 granny and 5 filet pieces chosen
- Size F/5/3.75mm crochet hook or size needed to obtain gauge
- Tapestry needle

GAUGE
Granny Squares before edgings = 3¾ inches square

PATTERN NOTE
Will be listed with each Square as needed.

SPECIAL STITCH
Will be listed with each Square as needed.

INSTRUCTIONS
SCARF
GRANNY SQUARE
MAKE 6.
Make 6 from the Granny Square Collection.

GRANNY SQUARE EDGING
Rnd 1: With RS facing, join with sc in corner ch sp, *[ch 1, sk next st, sc in next st] 7 times, ch 1, sk next st**, (sc, ch 2, sc) in next corner ch sp, rep from * around, ending last rep at **, sc in same corner ch sp as beg sc, ch 1, join with sc in beg sc, forming last ch sp.

Rnd 2: Ch 1, sc in ch sp just formed, *[sc in next st, sc in next ch] 8 times, sc in next st**, (sc, ch 2, sc) in next corner ch sp, rep from * around, ending last rep at **, sc in same ch sp as beg sc, ch 2, join with sl st in beg sc. Fasten off.

FILET RECTANGLES
MAKE 5.
Make 5 from the Filet Rectangle Collection.

FILET RECTANGLE EDGING
With RS facing, join with sc in top right corner open block, sc in same open block as joining sc, *[sc in next st, sc in next open block] 7 times, sc in next st, (2 sc, ch 2, 2 sc) in corner open block, [sc in next st, sc in next open block] 13 times, sc in next st*, (2 sc, ch 2, 2 sc) in next corner open block, rep between * once, 2 sc in same open block as joining sc, ch 2, join with sl st in beg sc. Fasten off.

ASSEMBLY
Beg and end with Granny Square, sew Granny Squares and Filet Rectangles alternately tog.

SCARF EDGING
With RS facing, join with sc in top right corner ch-2 sp, *[ch 1, sk next st, sc in next st] across, ending with ch 1, sk last st**, (sc, ch 2, sc) in next corner ch sp, rep from * around, ending last rep at **, sc in same corner ch sp as joining sc, ch 2, join with sl st in joining sc. Fasten off. ∎

Fingerless Gloves

SKILL LEVEL

INTERMEDIATE

FINISHED SIZES

Instructions given fit size X-small/small; changes for medium/large are in [ ].

MATERIALS

- Berroco Comfort DK light (DK) weight yarn (1¾ oz/178 yds/ 50g per ball):
  175 yds various colors of yarn for 4 granny and 2 filet pieces chosen for 1 pair of gloves
- Size F/5/3.75mm crochet hook or size needed to obtain gauge
- Tapestry needle
- Stitch markers

3 LIGHT

GAUGE

Granny Squares before edgings = 3¾ inches square

PATTERN NOTES

When working single crochet evenly around, one can work **single crochet decrease** *(see Stitch Guide)* as needed to avoid gaps.

When working fingers, gaps under chains can be sewn together if desired.

Chain-3 at beginning of row or round counts as first double crochet unless otherwise stated.

Join with slip stitch as indicated unless otherwise stated.

SPECIAL STITCHES

Double crochet cluster (dc cl): Holding back last lp of each st on hook, 2 dc as indicated in instructions, yo, pull through all lps on hook.

Single crochet cluster (sc cl): Holding back last lp of each st on hook, 2 sc as indicated in instructions, yo, pull through all lps on hook.

INSTRUCTIONS
GLOVE
MAKE 2.

Make 2 Granny Squares from Granny Square Collection.

X-SMALL/SMALL SIZE ONLY

With RS facing, join with sc in any corner ch sp, *sc in each of next 15 sts**, (sc, ch 1, sc) in next corner ch sp, rep from * around, ending last rep at **, sc in same ch sp as beg sc, ch 1, **join** *(see Pattern Notes)* in beg sc. Fasten off. *(68 sc)*

MEDIUM/LARGE SIZE ONLY

With RS facing, join in any corner ch sp, **ch 3** *(see Pattern Notes)*, dc in same ch sp as beg ch-3, *dc in each of next 15 sts**, (2 dc, ch 1, 2 dc) in next corner ch sp, rep from * around, ending last rep at **, 2 dc in same ch sp as beg ch-3, ch 1, join in 3rd ch of beg ch-3. Fasten off. *(76 dc)*

ASSEMBLY

With RS facing, sew 2 Granny Squares tog along one side edge, then with Squares still tog, sewing on opposite side, sew bottom *(mark for wrist)* corner ch-1 sp and next 5 [6] sts tog, then sew top *(mark for finger)* corner ch-1 sp and next 5 sts tog.

This leaves an opening of 7 [8] sts on each Granny Square for thumb.

Turn RS out.

FINGER EDGING

With RS facing, using Granny Square Edging color, join with sc at opening in top of glove, evenly sp 35 [37] sc around, join in beg sc. Fasten off. *(36 [38] sc)*

FINGER A

Rnd 1: Using color of choice join with sc at seam, sc in each of next 4 [5] sts, ch 2 [3], sk next 26 [27] sts, sc in each of last 5 sts, join in beg sc.

Rnd 2: Ch 1, sc in each st and in each ch around, join in beg sc. *(12 [14] sc)*

Rnd 3: Ch 1, **fpsc** *(see Stitch Guide)* around first st, **bpsc** *(see Stitch Guide)* around next st, [fpsc around next st, bpsc around next st] around, join in beg fpsc. Fasten off.

FINGER B

Rnd 1: Using color of choice, join with sc in next sk st, sc in each of next 3 sts, ch 2 [3], sk next 18 [19] sts, sc in each of next 4 sts, ch 2 [3], join in beg sc.

Rnds 2 & 3: Rep rnds 2 and 3 of Finger A.

FINGER C

Rnd 1: Using color of choice, join with sc in next sk st, sc in each of next 3 sts, ch 2 [3], sk next 10 [11] sts, sc in each of next 4 sts, ch 2 [3], join in beg sc.

Rnds 2 & 3: Rep rnds 2 and 3 of Finger A.

FINGER D

Rnd 1: Using color of choice, join with sc in next sk st, sc in each of next 9 [10] sts, ch 2 [3], join in beg sc.

Rnds 2 & 3: Rep rnds 2 and 3 of Finger A.

THUMB EDGING

With RS facing, using Granny Square Edging color, join with sc in opening on side of glove in st closest to Fingers, sc in each of next 6 [7] sts, **dc cl** *(see Special Stitches)* in joining seam, sc in each of next 7 [8] sts, **sc cl** *(see Special Stitches)* in joining seam, join in joining sc. Fasten off. *(16 [18] sts)*

THUMB

Rnd 1: Using color of choice, join with sc in st on thumb, sc in each of next 15 [17] sts, join in beg sc. *(16 [18] sc)*

Rnd 2: Ch 1, sc in each st around, join in beg sc.

Rnd 3: Ch 1, fpsc around first st, bpsc around next st, [fpsc around next st, bpsc around next st] around, join in beg fpsc. Fasten off.

WRIST RIBBING

Rnd 1: With RS facing, using Granny Square Edging color, join with sc in st farthest from thumb, evenly sp 29 [33] sc around, join in beg sc. *(30 [34] sc)*

Rnd 2: Mark 4 sts under Thumb, ch 1, fpsc around first st, bpsc around next st, [fpsc around next st, bpsc around next st] across to marker, in marked sts continue to work in est front post/back post pat using fpdc and bpdc sts, in rem sts on rnd, continue to work in est front post/back post pat using fpsc and bpsc sts, join in beg fpsc.

Rnd(s) 3 [3 & 4]: [Rep rnd 2] 1 [2] time(s). At end of last rnd, fasten off.

FILET

Work chosen chart from Filet in the Round 2 Collection around wrist opening. ■

Neck Warmer

SKILL LEVEL
INTERMEDIATE

FINISHED SIZE
22½ inches flat

MATERIALS
- Berroco Comfort DK light (DK) weight yarn (1¾ oz/178 yds/ 50g per ball):
  250 yds of various colors of yarn for 6 granny and 6 filet pieces chosen
- Size F/5/3.75mm crochet hook or size needed to obtain gauge
- Tapestry needle
- Buttons: 2

GAUGE
Granny Squares = 3¾ inches square

INSTRUCTIONS
NECKWARMER
GRANNY SQUARE
MAKE 6.
Make 6 from the Granny Square Collection.

ASSEMBLY
Sew Granny Squares tog side by side in long strip.

EDGING
With RS facing, join with sc in corner ch sp on bottom edge, sc in same ch sp as beg sc, *[sc in each of next 15 sts and chs, sc in next corner ch sp, sc in seam, sc in next corner ch sp on next Granny Square] 5 times, [sc in each of next 15 sts and chs**, (2 sc, ch 1, 2 sc) in next corner ch sp] twice, rep from * around, ending last rep at **, 2 sc in same ch sp as joining sc, ch 1, join with sl st in joining sc. Fasten off.

FILET FRINGE
Work 6 desired charts from Filet Fringe Collection, working in a continuous manner across bottom edge of Neck Warmer.

FINISHING
Sew 1 button in each corner at bottom of last Granny Square. Use corner ch sps of first Granny Square for buttonholes. ■

Headband

SKILL LEVEL

■■■▢
INTERMEDIATE

FINISHED SIZE
One size fits most.

MATERIALS
- Berroco Comfort DK light (DK) weight yarn (1¾ oz/178 yds/ 50g per ball):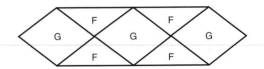
  150 yds various colors of yarn for 3 granny and 4 filet pieces chosen
- Size F/5/3.75mm crochet hook or size needed to obtain gauge
- Tapestry needle
- Sewing needle and thread
- 20-inch piece round cord elastic: 2

GAUGE
Granny Squares = 3¾ inches square

PATTERN NOTE
Join with slip stitch as indicated unless otherwise stated.

INSTRUCTIONS
HEADBAND
FILET HALF SQUARES
MAKE 4.
Work 4 Filet Half Squares from Filet Half Square Collection.

FILET HALF SQUARE EDGING
With RS facing, join with sc in last half open block made, sc in same half open block as joining sc, [sc in next st, 2 sc in next half open block] 5 times, sc in next st, (2 sc, ch 3, 2 sc) in next corner half open block, *[sc in next st, sc in next open block] 5 times, sc in next st*, (2 sc, ch 3, 2 sc) in corner open block, rep between * once, 2 sc in same half open block as joining sc, ch 3, **join** (see Pattern Note) in beg sc. Fasten off.

GRANNY SQUARE
MAKE 3.
Work 3 Granny Squares from Granny Square Collection.

ASSEMBLY
Sew Granny Squares and Filet Half Squares tog according to Assembly Diagram.

Headband Assembly Diagram

COLOR KEY
G Granny square
F Filet half square

HEADBAND EDGING
Form circle with each piece of elastic overlapping ends 1 inch, sew in place, forming 2 separate 19-inch rings.

With RS facing, join in end corner ch-3 sp on Granny Square, ch 1, working all sts over first ring of elastic, 2 sc in same corner as joining sl st, evenly sp sc across to other end corner ch-3 sp, 2 sc in corner ch-3 sp, drop first ring of elastic, ch 1, working over 2nd ring of elastic, 2 sc in same corner ch sp as last sc, evenly sp sc across to beg corner, 2 sc in same corner ch sp as beg sc, ch 1, join in beg sc. Fasten off. ■

Afghan
of Many
Colors

Afghan of Many Colors

SKILL LEVEL

INTERMEDIATE

FINISHED SIZE
48 inches square

MATERIALS
- Berroco Comfort DK light (DK) weight yarn (1¾ oz/178 yds/ 50g per ball): LIGHT
  8 balls MC for Granny Square Edging, Block Border, sewing and Afghan Border
  7 balls for Filet Squares
  1 ball each 8 various colors of yarn for Granny Squares
- Size F/5/3.75mm crochet hook or size needed to obtain gauge
- Tapestry needle

GAUGE
Granny Squares before edgings = 3¾ inches square

PATTERN NOTE
Join with slip stitch as indicated unless otherwise stated.

SPECIAL STITCH
Finishing join: With lp on hook, leaving long strand for sewing, fasten off, pull lp on hook up until yarn end comes through st. Insert hook from back to front through both lps of beg st on rnd, using hook, pull end through lps, insert hook from bottom to top of back lp of last ch made on rnd, using hook, pull end through lp forming the last corner ch on rnd and joining

INSTRUCTIONS
AFGHAN
GRANNY SQUARE
MAKE 48.
Make 48 from the Granny Square Collection using various colors.

GRANNY SQUARE EDGING
With RS facing, join with sc in corner ch sp, *sc in each of next 15 sts and chs**, (sc, ch 3, sc) in corner ch sp, rep from * around, ending last rep at **, sc in same ch sp as joining sc, ch 2, **finishing join** (see Special Stitch). Fasten off. (17 sts on each side edge)

BLOCK ASSEMBLY
Arrange 4 Squares to form twelve 2-Square x 2-Square pieces. Using Sewing Method, sew Squares in each column tog, forming 2 columns of 2 Squares, then sew columns tog.

SEWING METHOD
SEW SQUARES TOGETHER
Place 2 Squares tog with RS facing, using only outer lps of sts and chs, whipstitch pieces tog along 1 side starting with outer lp of 2nd ch in first ch-3 corner and ending outer lp of 2nd ch in last ch-3 corner.

SEW COLUMNS TOGETHER
Sew columns tog using same method as Sew Squares Together. When sewing where 2 Squares are joined, working ch-3 corners of current Squares, work whipstitch through outer lp of first ch, whipstitch through outer lp of 2nd ch, then working in ch-3 corners of next Squares, whipstitch through outer lp of 2nd ch, whipstitch through outer lp of 3rd ch.

GRANNY BLOCK BORDER

Rnd 1: With RS facing, join with sc in corner ch-3 sp, *sc in each of next 17 sts, dc dec (*see Stitch Guide*) in next corner sp on this Granny Square and in corner sp on next Granny Square, sc in each of next 17 sts**, (sc, ch 3, sc) in next corner ch sp, rep from * around, ending last rep at **, sc in same ch sp as joining sc, ch 1, dc in joining sc, forming last ch-3 sp. (*37 sts on each side edge*)

Rnd 2: Ch 1, sc in ch sp just formed, *[**fpdc** (*see Stitch Guide*) around next st, sc in next st] 18 times, fpdc around next st**, (sc, ch 3, sc) in next corner ch sp, rep from * around, ending last rep at **, sc in same ch sp as beg sc, ch 2, finishing join. Fasten off. (*39 sts on each side edge*)

FILET SQUARES
MAKE 13.
Make 13 from Filet Large Square Collection.

FILET EDGING

With RS facing and using the same color as Filet Square, join with sc in top right corner open block, sc in same corner open block as joining sc, *[sc in next st, sc in next open block] 15 times, sc in next st**, (2 sc, ch 3, 2 sc) in corner open block, rep from * around, ending last rep at **, 2 sc in same corner open block as joining sc, ch 3, join in joining sc. Fasten off. (*35 sts on each side edge*)

FILET BORDER

Rnd 1: With RS facing, join with sc in corner ch-3 sp, *sc in each of next 35 sts**, (sc, ch 3, sc) in corner ch sp, rep from * around, ending last rep at **, sc in same ch sp as joining sc, ch 1, dc in joining sc, forming last ch sp. (*37 sc on each side edge*)

Rnd 2: Ch 1, sc in ch sp just formed, *[fpdc around next st, sc in next st] 18 times, fpdc around next st**, (sc, ch 3, sc) in next corner ch sp, rep from * around, ending last rep at **, sc in same ch sp as beg sc, ch 2, finishing join. Fasten off. (*39 sts on each side edge*)

ASSEMBLY

Referring to Assembly Diagram, arrange Squares and Blocks to form 5 x 5-Square Afghan, beg with Filet Square in upper left corner, then alternating Filet and Granny Squares throughout.

Sew Squares and Blocks tog, forming 5 rows of 5 Squares then sew rows together.

AFGHAN OUTER BORDER

With RS facing and working in back lps, join with sc in last ch in corner ch-3 sp (*ch closest to the first sc*), *[sc in each of next 39 sts, dc dec in first ch in corner sp of this Square, in joining and in last ch of corner ch sp of next Square] 4 times, sc in each of next 39 sts**, sc in first ch, ch 3, sk next ch, sc in next ch (*corner*), rep from * around, ending last rep at **, sc in first ch of same corner ch sp as joining sc, ch 2, finishing join. Fasten off. ■

		37	47			24	7		
	F	30	41		F	2	50		F
38	1			37	12			26	15
13	18		F	8	11		F	12	43
		20	14			28	10		
	F	31	27		F	4	38		F
40	3			42	31			19	49
17	22		F	1	21		F	29	23
		27	4			39	2		
	F	10	50		F	3	25		F

Afghan
Assembly Diagram

Granny Square
Cardigan

SKILL LEVEL

INTERMEDIATE

FINISHED SIZES

Instructions given fit small/medium; changes for
large/X-large and 2X-large/3X-large are in [ ].

FINISHED GARMENT MEASUREMENTS

Bust: 41 inches *(small/medium)* [51 inches *(large/
X-large)*, 61 inches *(2X-large/3X-large)*]

MATERIALS

- Berroco Comfort DK light (DK)
  weight yarn (1¾ oz/178 yds/
  50g per ball):
      6 [8, 10] balls various colors
      for Granny Squares
      6 [8, 10] balls MC for Filet Squares,
      Edgings and Collar
- Size F/5/3.75mm crochet hook
  or size needed to obtain gauge
- Tapestry needle
- 1⅛-inch button

GAUGE

Granny Square before edging =
  3¾ inches square

PATTERN NOTES

Join with slip stitch as indicated unless
  otherwise stated.

Chain-3 at beginning of row or round counts as
  first double crochet unless otherwise stated.

Chain-4 at beginning of row or round counts
  as first double crochet and corner chain-1 sp
  unless otherwise stated.

INSTRUCTIONS
CARDIGAN
GRANNY SQUARES
MAKE 44 [54, 72].

Make 44 [54, 72] from the Granny Square
  Collection using various colors.

ASSEMBLY
FRONT AND BACK OF CARDIGAN

After First Granny Square Edging is worked,
  crochet remaining squares to previously
  edged Granny Squares, according to Assembly
  Diagram on page 84.

SLEEVES

Crochet 3 [4, 4] Granny Squares to each arm
  opening for top of sleeve, crochet 3 [4, 4]
  Granny Squares to each top of sleeve opening
  for bottom of sleeve.

FIRST GRANNY SQUARE EDGING

Rnd 1: With RS facing, **join** *(see Pattern Notes)*
  MC in corner ch sp, **ch 3** *(see Pattern Notes)*, dc
  in same ch sp as beg ch-3, *dc in each of next 15
  sts and chs**, (2 dc, ch 3, 2 dc) in corner ch sp,
  rep from * around, ending last rep at **, 2 dc in
  same corner ch sp as beg ch-3, ch 1, dc in 3rd ch
  of beg ch-3, forming corner ch sp.

Rnd 2: Ch 3, sl st in corner ch sp just formed,
  *[ch 3, sk next 3 dc, sl st in next dc] 4 times, ch
  3, sk next 3 dc**, (sl st, ch 3, sl st) in corner ch
  sp, rep from * around, ending last rep at **, sl st
  in same ch sp as beg sl st, join in first ch of beg
  ch-3. Fasten off.

GRANNY SQUARE EDGING JOINING ON 1 SIDE

Rnd 1: Rep rnd 1 of First Granny Square Edging.

Rnd 2: Ch 1, sl st in corner ch-3 sp of previous Granny Square, ch 1, sl st in same ch sp on this Granny Square as beg ch-1, [ch 1, sl st in next ch-3 sp on previous Granny Square, ch 1, sk next 3 dc on this Granny Square, sl st in next st] 5 times (last sl st will be in corner ch-3 sp of this Granny Square), ch 1, sl st in corner ch-3 sp on previous Granny Square, ch 1, sl st in corner ch-3 sp on this Granny Square, *[ch 3, sk next 3 dc, sl st in next dc] 4 times, ch 3, sk next 3 dc**, (sl st ch3, sl st) in corner ch sp, rep from * around, ending last rep at **, join in beg ch-1. Fasten off.

GRANNY SQUARE EDGING JOINING ON 2 SIDES

Rnd 1: Rep rnd 1 of First Granny Square Edging.

Rnd 2: Ch 1, sl st in corner ch-3 sp of previous Granny Square, ch 1, sl st in same ch sp on this Granny Square as beg ch-1, *[ch 1, sl st in next ch-3 sp on previous Granny Square, ch 1, sk next 3 dc on this Granny Square, sl st in next st] 5 times (last sl st will be in corner ch-3 sp of this Granny Square)*, sl st in corner sp on previous Granny Square, ch 1, sl st in corner sp on next previous Granny Square, sl st in corner sp on this Granny Square, rep between * once, ch 1, sl st in corner ch-3 sp on previous Granny Square, ch 1, sl st in corner sp on this Granny Square, **[ch 3, sk next 3 dc, sl st in next st] 4 times, ch 3, sk next 3 dc***, (sl st, ch 3, sl st), in corner ch sp, rep from ** twice, ending last rep at ***, join in beg ch-1. Fasten off.

GRANNY SQUARE EDGING
JOINING ON 3 SIDES
Rnd 1: Rep rnd 1 of First Granny Square Edging.

Rnd 2: Ch 1, sl st in corner ch-3 sp of previous Granny Square, ch 1, sl st in same ch sp on this Granny Square as beg ch-1, *[ch 1, sl st in next ch-3 sp on previous Granny Square, ch 1, sk next 3 dc on this Granny Square, sl st in next st] 5 times (*last sl st will be in corner ch-3 sp of this Granny Square*)**, sl st in corner sp on previous Granny Square, ch 1, sl st in corner sp on next previous Granny Square, sl st in corner sp on this Granny Square, rep from * joining 3 sides, ending last rep at **, ch 1, sl st in corner ch-3 sp on previous Granny Square, ch 1, sl st in corner sp on this Granny Square, [ch 3, sk next 3 dc, sl st in next st] 4 times, ch 3, sk next 3 dc, join in beg ch-1. Fasten off.

HALF GRANNY SQUARE
MAKE 2.
Row 1 (RS): Ch 4, sl st in first ch to form ring, **ch 4** (*see Pattern Notes*), 3 dc in ring, ch 3 (*corner*), 3 dc in ring, ch 1 (*corner*), dc in ring. Fasten off.

Row 2: With RS facing, join any color in any ch-1 corner ch sp, ch 4, 3 dc in same corner ch sp as beg ch-4, ch 1, (3 dc, ch 3, 3 dc) in ch-3 corner ch sp, ch 1, (3 dc, ch 1, dc) in corner ch-1 sp. Fasten off.

Row 3: With RS facing, join any color in corner ch-1 sp, ch 4, 3 dc in same corner ch-1 sp as beg ch-4, ch 1, 3 dc in next ch-1 sp, ch 1, (3 dc, ch 3, 3 dc) in next corner ch-3 sp, ch 1, 3 dc in next ch-1 sp, ch 1, (3 dc, ch 1, dc) in corner ch-1 sp. Fasten off.

Row 4: With RS facing, join any color in corner ch-1 sp, ch 4, 3 dc in same corner ch sp as beg ch-4, [ch 1, 3 dc in next ch-1 sp] twice, ch 1, (3 dc, ch 3, 3 dc) in corner ch-3 sp, [ch 1, 3 dc in next ch-1 sp] twice, ch 1, (3 dc, ch 1, dc) in corner ch-1 sp. Fasten off.

HALF GRANNY SQUARE EDGING
JOINING ON 2 SIDES
Rnd 1: With RS facing, join MC in corner ch-1 sp, ch 3, dc in same ch sp as beg ch-3, dc in each of next 15 sts and chs, (2 dc, ch 3, 2 dc) in next corner ch-3 sp, dc in each of next 15 sts or chs,

2 dc in next corner ch-1 sp, ch 3, 2 dc in side of last dc, evenly sp 19 dc across ends of rows to next corner, 2 dc in side of beg ch-3, ch 1, dc in 3rd ch of beg ch-3, forming last corner ch sp.

Rnd 2: Ch 1, sl st in corner ch-3 sp of previous Granny Square, ch 1, sl st in same ch sp as beg ch-1, *[ch 1, sl st in next ch-3 sp on previous Granny Square, ch 1, sk next 3 dc on Half Granny Square, sl st in next st] 5 times (*last sl st will be in corner ch of Half Granny Square*)*, sl st in corner ch-3 sp of previous Granny Square, ch 1, sl st in corner ch-3 sp of next Granny Square, sl st in same corner ch sp as last sl st on Half Granny Square, rep between * once, ch 1, sl st in corner ch-3 sp of last Granny Square joined in, ch 1, sl st in same corner ch sp as last sl st on Half Granny Square, [ch 3, sk next 3 dc on Half Granny Square, sl st in next dc] 5 times, ch 3, sk next 3 dc, join in beg ch-1. Fasten off.

FRONT & BOTTOM EDGING
Row 1: With RS facing, working under Half Granny Square on left side, join MC in top corner ch-3 sp on Granny Square, ch 3, sl st in same corner ch sp as beg sl st, *[ch 3, sl st in next ch-3 sp] 5 times, ch 3**, sk next corner ch-3 sp, sl st between corner ch-3 sp of current Granny Square and corner ch-3 sp of next Granny Square, sk corner ch-3 sp of next Granny Square, rep from * across to bottom of left front, ending last rep at **, (sl st, ch 3, sl st) in corner ch-3 sp, continue working ch-3 sps in same manner to top corner ch-3 sp on Granny Square under Half Granny Square on right side, working (sl st, ch 3, sl st) in next bottom corner and in last corner, turn.

Row 2: Sl st in corner ch-3 sp just made, [ch 3, sl st in next ch-3 sp] across to bottom of right front, (sl st, ch 3, sl st) in corner ch-3 sp, continue working ch-3 sps in same manner to top of left side with (sl st, ch 3, sl st) in next bottom corner, turn.

Row 3: Ch 3, sl st in first ch-3 sp, [ch 3, sl st in next ch-3 sp] across to bottom of left front, (sl st, ch 3, sl st) in next ch-3 sp, continue working ch-3 sps in like manner to top of right side with (sl st, ch 3, sl st) in next bottom corner ch sp and in last corner ch sp. Fasten off.

COLLAR

Row 1: Mark 6 turns as shown on Assembly Diagram on page 84, with RS facing, join MC in last corner ch-3 sp made on Front and Bottom Edging, ch 1, evenly sp sc in multiples of 4 plus 1 across neck opening working **sc dec** (*see Stitch Guide*) in each turn to round neck opening, turn.

Row 2: Ch 1, 2 sc in first st, sc in each st across, working sc dec in each of 6 marked turns to round neck opening, ending with 2 sc in last st, turn.

Rows 3 & 4: Rep row 2.

Row 5: Remove marker at first and last turns, ch 1, 2 sc in first st, ch 4, sk next 4 sts (*buttonhole*), sc in next st, sc in each st across to last st, working sc dec in each of 4 marked turns to round neck opening, ending with 2 sc in last st, turn.

Row 6: Ch 1, 2 sc in first st, sc in each st and ch across to last st, working sc dec in each of 4 marked turns to round neck opening, ending with 2 sc in last st, turn.

Rows 7 & 8: Rep row 6.

Row 9: [Ch 3, sk next 3 sts, sl st in next st] across. Fasten off.

Sew button to Collar opposite buttonhole.

SLEEVE FILET
MAKE 2.

Rnd 1: With RS facing, join MC in sp between 2 Granny Square corners, *ch 3, sk next corner ch-3 sp, sl st in next ch-3 sp, [ch 3, sl st in next ch-3 sp] 4 times, ch 3, sk next corner ch-3 sp**, sl st between corner ch-3 sp of this Granny Square and corner ch-3 sp of next Granny Square, rep from * around, ending last rep at **, join in first ch of beg ch-3.

Rnd 2: Sl st in ch-3 sp, ch 4, (dc, ch 1) twice in same ch sp as beg ch-4, (dc, ch 1) 3 times in each ch-3 sp around, join in 3rd ch of beg ch-4. (54 [72, 72] ch-1 sps)

Next rnds: Work Filet of choice from Filet in the Round 1 Collection.

SLEEVE EDGING

Rnd 1: [Ch 3, sk next ch, sl st in next dc] around, ch 3, join in joining sl st of last rnd.

Rnd 2: Sl st in ch-3 sp, [ch 3, sl st in next ch-3 sp] around, ch 3, join in beg sl st.

Rnd 3: Rep rnd 2. Fasten off.

Rep on rem Sleeve. ■

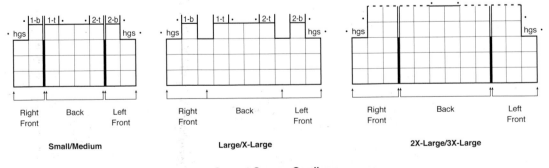

Granny Square Cardigan
Assembly Diagram
On size S/M and L/XL, squares with matching numerical numbers are folded halves of the same square—t (top) and b (bottom).
On size 2XL/3XL, crochet matching colored dotted lines together for shoulder seams.
hgs—shows Half Granny Square Placement.
• Indicate turns where decreases are worked when working Collar.

STITCH GUIDE

FOR MORE COMPLETE INFORMATION, VISIT **FREEPATTERNS.COM**

STITCH ABBREVIATIONS

beg . . . . begin/begins/beginning
bpdc . . . . back post double crochet
bpsc . . . . back post single crochet
bptr . . . . back post treble crochet
CC . . . . contrasting color
ch(s) . . . . chain(s)
ch- . . . . refers to chain or space
previously made (i.e., ch-1 space)
ch sp(s) . . . . chain space(s)
cl(s) . . . . cluster(s)
cm . . . . centimeter(s)
dc . . . . double crochet (singular/plural)
dc dec . . . . double crochet 2 or more
stitches together, as indicated
dec . . . . decrease/decreases/decreasing
dtr . . . . double treble crochet
ext . . . . extended
fpdc . . . . front post double crochet
fpsc . . . . front post single crochet
fptr . . . . front post treble crochet
g . . . . gram(s)
hdc . . . . half double crochet
hdc dec . . . . half double crochet 2 or more
stitches together, as indicated
inc . . . . increase/increases/increasing
lp(s) . . . . loop(s)
MC . . . . main color
mm . . . . millimeter(s)
oz . . . . ounce(s)
pc . . . . popcorn(s)
rem . . . . remain/remains/remaining
rep(s) . . . . repeat(s)
rnd(s) . . . . round(s)
RS . . . . right side
sc . . . . single crochet (singular/plural)
sc dec . . . . single crochet 2 or more
stitches together, as indicated
sk . . . . skip/skipped/skipping
sl st(s) . . . . slip stitch(es)
sp(s) . . . . space(s)/spaced
st(s) . . . . stitch(es)
tog . . . . together
tr . . . . treble crochet
trtr . . . . triple treble
WS . . . . wrong side
yd(s) . . . . yard(s)
yo . . . . yarn over

YARN CONVERSION

OUNCES TO GRAMS		GRAMS TO OUNCES	
1	28.4	25	7⁄8
2	56.7	40	1²⁄₃
3	85.0	50	1¾
4	113.4	100	3½

UNITED STATES / UNITED KINGDOM

UNITED STATES		UNITED KINGDOM
sl st (slip stitch)	=	sc (single crochet)
sc (single crochet)	=	dc (double crochet)
hdc (half double crochet)	=	htr (half treble crochet)
dc (double crochet)	=	tr (treble crochet)
tr (treble crochet)	=	dtr (double treble crochet)
dtr (double treble crochet)	=	ttr (triple treble crochet)
skip	=	miss

Reverse single crochet (reverse sc): Ch 1, sk first st, working from left to right, insert hook in next st from front to back, draw up lp on hook, yo, and draw through both lps on hook.

Chain (ch): Yo, pull through lp on hook.

Single crochet (sc): Insert hook in st, yo, pull through st, yo, pull through both lps on hook.

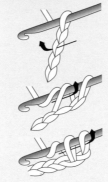

Double crochet (dc): Yo, insert hook in st, yo, pull through st, [yo, pull through 2 lps] twice.

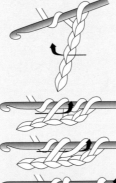

Front loop (front lp) Back loop (back lp)
Front Loop   Back Loop

Front post stitch (fp): Back post stitch (bp): When working post st, insert hook from right to left around post of st on previous row.

Back   Front

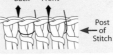

Post of Stitch

Half double crochet (hdc): Yo, insert hook in st, yo, pull through st, yo, pull through all 3 lps on hook.

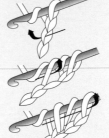

Double treble crochet (dtr): Yo 3 times, insert hook in st, yo, pull through st, [yo, pull through 2 lps] 4 times.

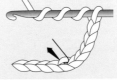

Slip stitch (sl st): Insert hook in st, pull through both lps on hook.

Chain color change (ch color change) Yo with new color, draw through last lp on hook.

Double crochet color change (dc color change) Drop first color, yo with new color, draw through last 2 lps of st.

Treble crochet (tr): Yo twice, insert hook in st, yo, pull through st, [yo, pull through 2 lps] 3 times.

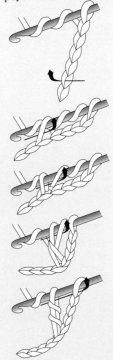

Single crochet decrease (sc dec): (Insert hook, yo, draw lp through) in each of the sts indicated, yo, draw through all lps on hook.

Example of 2-sc dec

Half double crochet decrease (hdc dec): (Yo, insert hook, yo, draw lp through) in each of the sts indicated, yo, draw through all lps on hook.

Example of 2-hdc dec

Double crochet decrease (dc dec): (Yo, insert hook, yo, draw lp through, yo, draw through 2 lps on hook) in each of the sts indicated, yo, draw through all lps on hook.

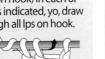

Example of 2-dc dec

Treble crochet decrease (tr dec): Holding back last lp of each st, tr in each of the sts indicated, yo, pull through all lps on hook.

Example of 2-tr dec

Metric
Conversion
Charts

METRIC CONVERSIONS

yards	x	.9144	=	metres (m)
yards	x	91.44	=	centimetres (cm)
inches	x	2.54	=	centimetres (cm)
inches	x	25.40	=	millimetres (mm)
inches	x	.0254	=	metres (m)

centimetres	x	.3937	=	inches
metres	x	1.0936	=	yards

INCHES INTO MILLIMETRES & CENTIMETRES (Rounded off slightly)

inches	mm	cm	inches	cm	inches	cm	inches	cm
1/8	3	0.3	5	12.5	21	53.5	38	96.5
1/4	6	0.6	5 1/2	14	22	56	39	99
3/8	10	1	6	15	23	58.5	40	101.5
1/2	13	1.3	7	18	24	61	41	104
5/8	15	1.5	8	20.5	25	63.5	42	106.5
3/4	20	2	9	23	26	66	43	109
7/8	22	2.2	10	25.5	27	68.5	44	112
1	25	2.5	11	28	28	71	45	114.5
1 1/4	32	3.2	12	30.5	29	73.5	46	117
1 1/2	38	3.8	13	33	30	76	47	119.5
1 3/4	45	4.5	14	35.5	31	79	48	122
2	50	5	15	38	32	81.5	49	124.5
2 1/2	65	6.5	16	40.5	33	84	50	127
3	75	7.5	17	43	34	86.5		
3 1/2	90	9	18	46	35	89		
4	100	10	19	48.5	36	91.5		
4 1/2	115	11.5	20	51	37	94		

KNITTING NEEDLES CONVERSION CHART

Canada/U.S.	0	1	2	3	4	5	6	7	8	9	10	10½	11	13	15
Metric (mm)	2	2¼	2¾	3¼	3½	3¾	4	4½	5	5½	6	6½	8	9	10

CROCHET HOOKS CONVERSION CHART

Canada/U.S.	1/B	2/C	3/D	4/E	5/F	6/G	8/H	9/I	10/J	10½/K	N
Metric (mm)	2.25	2.75	3.25	3.5	3.75	4.25	5	5.5	6	6.5	9.0

RETAIL STORES: If you would like to carry this pattern book or any other DRG publications, visit DRGwholesale.com

Every effort has been made to ensure that the instructions in this publication are complete and accurate. We cannot, however, take responsibility for human error, typographical mistakes or variations in individual work. Please visit AnniesCustomerCare.com to check for pattern updates.

Library of Congress Control Number: 2011961135

ISBN: 978-1-59635-421-0

1 2 3 4 5 6 7 8 9